THE MATERIAL
OF KNOWLEDGE

THE MATERIAL
OF KNOWLEDGE

FEMINIST DISCLOSURES

SUSAN HEKMAN

Indiana University Press
Bloomington and Indianapolis

This book is a publication of

Indiana University Press
601 North Morton Street
Bloomington, Indiana 47404-3797 USA

www.iupress.indiana.edu

Telephone orders 800-842-6796
Fax orders   812-855-7931
Orders by e-mail iuporder@indiana.edu

♾ The paper used in this publication meets the minimum requirements of the American National Standard for Information Sciences—Permanence of Paper for Printed Library Materials, ANSI Z39.48-1992.

Manufactured in the United States of America

Library of Congress Cataloging-in-Publication Data

Hekman, Susan J.
   The material of knowledge : feminist disclosures / Susan Hekman.
      p. cm.
   Includes bibliographical references and index.
   ISBN 978-0-253-35467-9 (cloth : alk. paper) — ISBN 978-0-253-22196-4 (pbk. : alk. paper)   1. Philosophy, Modern—21st century.   2. Civilization, Modern—21st century.   3. Feminist theory.   I. Title.
   B805.H45 2010
   108.2—dc22
                                                             2009045455

1   2   3   4   5   15   14   13   12   11   10

In memory of Buzz

CONTENTS

ACKNOWLEDGMENTS

This book is an extension of the article published in the volume that I edited with Stacy Alaimo (*Material Feminisms*, Indiana University Press, 2008). I owe an immense debt to Stacy for introducing me to this literature and, in effect, opening up a whole new world. The intellectual and personal interaction between us on this project was truly extraordinary. Both professionally and personally, Stacy has given me an invaluable gift.

During the writing of this book my husband of twenty-five years, Evan (Buzz) Anders, died. Although he never got to see the end result, this book is his in a profound sense. For the years we were together, he inspired and encouraged me in every way imaginable. I miss him deeply.

Stacy Alaimo and Timothy Luke read and commented on an earlier draft of the manuscript. Many thanks to them for helping me improve it. And, finally, thanks go to my equine companions, Justin and Pepper, who gave me love and laughs when I needed it most.

THE MATERIAL
OF KNOWLEDGE

INTRODUCTION

The first years of the twenty-first century seem to be characterized by events with overwhelming material consequences. Terrorist attacks, tsunamis, hurricanes, tornadoes, and earthquakes dominate the news. The death toll mounts, and we brace ourselves for the next disaster. Commentary on these disasters is certainly not lacking. Yet the commentaries emerging from the academic community are curiously devoid of insight.[1] Since the linguistic turn of the mid-twentieth century, the academic world has been focused on language, and particularly on its constitutive power. Language, it is agreed, constitutes the reality that we as humans inhabit. It constitutes our social world and the structures that define it. It also constitutes the natural world by providing us with concepts that structure that world. We humans, in short, are the creators of all we survey.

Linguistic constructionism, however, has trouble with matter. Did our concepts constitute the tsunami that devastated parts of Asia? Or hurricane Katrina's destruction of New Orleans? Or, even more disturbingly, the attack on the Twin Towers? The linguistic constructionists tell us that we understand all of these events linguistically and that it is this understanding that constitutes their reality. Yet something is missing in this explanation. Something happened in these events—and by extension all events—that escapes the strictly linguistic. Human and nonhuman entities were destroyed. Lives were lost. Matter manifested itself. It is undoubtedly true that we understand our world linguistically. But what this leaves out is that there is a world out there that we understand. Dogmatic adherence to linguistic constitution cannot account for the reality and agency of that world.

The story I want to tell in this book begins with modernity and the reaction to modernity loosely categorized as linguistic (or social) constructionism. But most importantly, it is a story about where we go from here. As the devastating material events of the last few years have illustrated, we need a new conception to understand the world in which we live. The question I want to explore is what that conception will look like. If we reject modernity and the linguistic constructionism of approaches such as postmodernism, what do we have left? What are our options? What alternatives are left to us to explain a world that escapes our current theoretical approaches? My goal here is not to present a survey of modernity and postmodernism. Rather, it is to present and defend three theses: first, that we are currently witnessing a sea change in intellectual thought; second, that feminism is at the forefront of this sea change; and third, that our goal at this point must be to define an alternative approach that brings the material back in.

The principal characteristic of the sea change we are now witnessing is a reaction against linguistic constructionism. Theorists from across the intellectual spectrum are finding linguistic constructionism inadequate. Specifically, they are finding that linguistic constructionism's loss of the material, its inability to bring the material dimension into theory and practice, its inability to talk about anything except language, imposes an unacceptable constraint on theory. A central aspect of this sea change, however, is the equally strong conviction that we must not return to the approach to the material embodied in modernity. Modernity was all about matter. For modernists the aim of philosophy was to get matter right, to develop concepts that mirror nature. The virtue of linguistic constructionism was to show the error of this approach. Linguistic constructionists revealed that matter and language/discourse are inseparable. They showed that the goal of "pure" knowledge of matter strictly separated from language is misguided.

One way of characterizing the shift I am trying to describe is to put it in terms of the reality/language dichotomy. Modernity chose the reality side of the dichotomy, defining its goal as the accurate depiction of reality. The linguistic constructionists chose the language side, insisting that since language constitutes reality we don't need to talk about anything except language. Characterizing the situation this way puts the postmoderns in an awkward position. It is central to the postmoderns' position, if indeed postmodernism can be said to have a center, that postmodernism deconstructs dichotomies. Yet in practice most postmoderns have failed to deconstruct this crucial dichotomy. Instead, they have moved to the language side to the exclusion of reality. Postmoderns don't like to talk about reality because of its modernist association. So they simply ignore it.

The challenge that confronts us, then, is to do what the postmoderns claim but fail to do: to deconstruct the language/reality dichotomy by defining a theoretical position that does not privilege either language or reality but instead explains and builds on their intimate interaction.[2] That accomplishing this goal in the present intellectual climate is a difficult task should go without saying. Linguistic constructionism is deeply imbedded in the academic culture. The theorists that I discuss here, however, provide the basis for a new definition. My strategy has two trajectories. On the one hand, I reinterpret the work of Wittgenstein and Foucault, two theorists commonly identified as architects of linguistic constructionism, and argue that their work is better understood as articulating the interconnection of language and reality. On the other hand, I build on the work of contemporary theorists such as Latour, Pickering, Tuana, and Barad who are explicitly seeking another way. In both cases my goal is to move toward a better articulation of this new theoretical position.

My second thesis is that feminist thought has been and continues to be in the forefront of this sea change. Feminist theorists have a particular stake in retaining reference to reality. Feminists want to be able to make statements about reality—that women are oppressed; that their social, economic, and political status is inferior to that of men; that they suffer sexual abuse at the hands of men. If everything is a linguistic construction, then these claims lose their meaning. They become only one more interpretation of an infinitely malleable reality. Moreover, feminists have been and continue to be concerned about the reality of women's bodies. We want to be able to talk about women's pain, their biology, the effect of medications and toxins on women's bodies. Once more, linguistic constructionism precludes this. My contention is that feminist theory has begun the difficult process of articulating a new approach to the relationship between language and reality, and furthermore, that we will continue to learn much from feminism as this process unfolds. Feminist theory is the focus of this book for both of these reasons. Feminists have, in a sense, pointed us in the right direction as we attempt to define a new theoretical approach. And feminist thought will shape that new approach in fundamental ways.

My third thesis is that what we need at this point is not another critique of linguistic constructionism but a concerted effort to define an alternative approach that brings the material back in. This approach must incorporate the insights of linguistic constructionism without falling into its error of rejecting the material. It must describe the complex interactions of language and matter, the human and the nonhuman, as well as the diverse entities we have created in our world. It must be able to explain the interactions and even agencies of these entities without retreating to the modernist mirror of nature. Although critiques of linguistic constructionism abound in contemporary discussions, what is lacking is the articulation of an alternative approach. It is my contention that this is what is required if we are to move out of the theoretical impasse in which we find ourselves.

The nature of that theoretical impasse was perhaps most bluntly stated in an article by Bruno Latour in *Critical Inquiry* in 2004. The editors of *Critical Inquiry* asked a set of prominent theorists to discuss the future of critical theory in an essay. Latour's answer was particularly crucial in this context because he has been closely associated for several decades with one of the major components of critical theory and a key element of constructionism: social studies of scientific knowledge. Latour was one of the pioneers of the movement that studies science as a social construction and argued that the concepts of science are constitutive of the reality scientists study. But after several decades of the social studies of science, Latour came to question whether the constructionist path is the correct one for critical theory. He came to the conclusion that it was an error to believe that there was no way to criticize matters of fact except by moving away from them and analyzing the conditions that made them possible.

> My argument is that a certain form of critical spirit has sent us down the wrong path, encouraging us to fight the wrong enemies and, worst of all, to be considered friends by the wrong sort of allies because of a little mistake in the definition of its main target. The question was never to get *away* from facts but closer to them, not fighting empiricism but, on the contrary, renewing empiricism. (2004:231)

Latour also offers an assessment of what we need to do to correct these errors. What is required, he asserts, is a "second empiricism," new critical tools, a new critical attitude:

> not a flight into the conditions of possibility of a given matter of fact, not the addition of something more human that the inhumane matters of fact would have missed, but, rather, a multifarious inquiry launched with the tools of anthropology, philosophy, metaphysics, history, sociology to detect *how many participants* are gathered in a *thing* to make it exist and maintain its existence. (2004:245–46)

The critic, in short, should not be one who debunks, but one who assembles.

The story that Latour tells in this article, the tale of how critical theory went down the wrong path despite the best of intentions, is clearly evident in the history of recent feminist theory. Like Latour, feminist theorists were fascinated by social construction. They embraced the social constructionist thesis that facts are constructed, not discovered. Social constructionism provides an invaluable tool for explaining the workings of the social structures that create and maintain the subordination of women. As a consequence, social constructionism became the centerpiece of feminist theory for several decades. But feminists, like Latour, never meant to reject the reality they studied, to move away from the material in favor of the discursive. Rather, their intent was to better understand material reality. For feminists, the baseline has always been the reality of women's situation and an attempt to understand that reality and alleviate the pain it causes. But as with the situation of science studies that Latour describes, things did not work out as intended.

The work of Donna Haraway exemplifies the dilemma of feminist theory that ensued. Haraway, like Latour, was a pioneer in the social constructionist movement in science studies. Her pathbreaking analysis of primatology revealed how race and sexuality are written into the definition of nature in twentieth-century Western science (1989). Her application of social constructionism in science studies debunked the objective reality of nature in primatology. She revealed how the masculinist concepts of the field created a masculine world of apes and women in which nature was gendered and raced.

But Haraway's intent was never to remove herself or feminist theory from the real world. Like others engaged in social studies of science, her goal was to understand the reality she studied, not to obliterate it. This intention is clearly evident in her influential essay "A Manifesto for Cyborgs" (1990). The aim of her article, Haraway states, is to "build an ironic political myth faithful to feminism, socialism, and materialism" (1990:190). Many of the themes that will dominate subsequent feminist thought are here. First, the cyborg: a cybernetic organism, a hybrid of machine and organism, a creature of social reality and fiction. By the late twentieth century, Haraway argues, we are all cyborgs: "The cyborg is our ontology; it gives us our politics." Second, there is social reality: "lived social relations, our most important political construct, a world-changing fiction" (1990:191).

This, according to Haraway, is the world we face. It is a world of cyborgs, a world that breaks down the binaries of human/animal, organism/machine, physical/non-physical. In this world, Haraway argues, we need a new political myth for socialist feminism. Although she does not say so explicitly, Haraway implies that the old myth, the Marxist myth of an objective reality, is no longer applicable. We need a new approach that can not only deal with cyborgs but can combine fact and fiction into a political conception. But at the outset, Haraway also realizes that there is a danger in taking the path she has described: "We risk lapsing into boundless difference and giving up on the confusing task of making partial, real connections" (1990:202).

The task that Haraway sets for feminism, then, is a difficult one. She wants to formulate a politics rooted in claims about fundamental change in the nature of class, race, and gender in an emerging world order (1990:203). She wants this conception to understand discursive constructions as "no joke." And she wants a conception that is not anti–science and technology but that nevertheless understands them as a matrix of complex dominations. Science and technology, she asserts, provide fresh sources of power; we need fresh sources of analyses and political action to meet this power (1990:207).

In hindsight, it seems fair to conclude that Haraway's vision has not been realized. Instead of deconstructing the discourse/reality dichotomy, instead of constructing a new paradigm for feminism that integrates the discursive and the material, feminism has instead turned to the discursive pole of the discourse/reality dichotomy. Inspired by theorists such as Haraway who revealed the discursive constitution of scientific "reality" and by postmodern theorists who examined the discursive constitution of social reality, many feminists turned to discourse at the expense of the material. Haraway's desire to define a feminist discourse of materialism was lost in the linguistic turn of feminism and critical theory as a whole. It is significant that Haraway's article is reprinted and reaches its widest audience in a volume, *Feminism/Postmodernism* (Nicholson 1990), that examines the question of the relevance of postmodernism for feminism. By the time the volume was published, the question was already moot: postmodernism had transformed feminism.

But although Haraway's goal of a new materialism has not been realized in feminist theory, discontent with the linguistic turn in feminism has been evident from the outset. Early on, Christine Di Stefano complained about "The Incredible Shrinking Woman" (1987). Susan Bordo challenged Judith Butler's turn away from the material and argued that the materiality of the body must be at the center of feminist theory (Bordo 1998). Nancy Tuana took on the fundamental dichotomy of nature/nurture (1983). Other feminists tried to articulate a concept of identity more substantial than the postmodern's fictional self (Valverde 2004; Moya and Hames-Garcia 2000; Hekman 2004). A number of feminist philosophers argued that analytic philosophy should not be dismissed out of hand by feminists because of its association with modernity (Antony and Witt 2002).

In retrospect it seems obvious that the discontent with the linguistic turn and social constructionism that Latour expresses so bluntly has been building for some time. Feminists are not alone. Philosophers, never enthusiastic about postmodernism, have engaged in seemingly endless debates about relativism, realism, and anti-realism. Philosophers of science, who quite obviously have a stake in the material world, have objected to the loss of that world. Given the gathering objections to social constructionism/the linguistic turn, one wonders why it gained such popularity in the first place. There is a very simple answer to this question: it reveals a profound truth about human knowledge. Linguistic constructionists were right about one important point: human knowledge is constructed by human concepts. It is of overwhelming importance that we do not abandon this insight. The challenge posed by the linguistic turn will not be met by a return to modernity. Rather, we must fashion an approach that brings the material back in without rejecting the legitimate insights of the linguistic turn.

It is easy to criticize the excesses of the linguistic turn. What is difficult is articulating a new theoretical position that meets the challenge of the linguistic turn. The purpose of this book is to do precisely this: to move the discussion toward a clearer articulation of a new theoretical approach. The framework I will use for my discussion is a concept developed by Bruno Latour: the new settlement. Latour argues that our task today must be to arrive at a "new settlement" that resolves the fundamental issues of language and reality posed by modernity (1999b:81). Although Latour would be the first to admit that his new theoretical approach needs much development, his work has the advantage of providing a clear understanding of what this new approach should look like.

In his 1993 book, *We Have Never Been Modern,* Latour poses a challenge to social constructionism in science:

> Are you not fed up at finding yourself forever locked into language alone, or imprisoned in social representations alone, as so many social scientists would like you to be? (1993:90)

Postmodernism, Latour claims, is a symptom not a solution. The problem is what he calls the "modernist settlement," the assumption that nature and society, science and politics, are and must be kept separate. Latour's analysis of this settlement appears contradictory. He asserts, first, that "we have never been modern," that is, that the attempt to separate society and nature was doomed to failure from the start. He also asserts, however, that our attempt to be modern, to effect this separation, has skewed our understanding of what is at stake and distorted our attempts to find a new settlement that better describes our situation. The contradiction of trying to be what we never can be, in other words, has complicated our attempts to find another way.

Building on Latour's insight, I will argue here that there are a number of versions of the new settlement emerging in contemporary discussions. My goal is to build on and add to these settlements as a way of moving toward a clearer understanding of an alternative conception. The first settlement I will discuss has its origins in the philosophy of science. Theorists such as Latour and, especially, Andrew Pickering are formulating an approach to our relationship not only to language and reality but also to the other entities that comprise our world. This settlement springs from the influential social studies of scientific knowledge that have transformed science studies, but it also departs from this tradition in significant ways. The second settlement has its origins in the work of analytic philosophers. Focusing on the work of Wittgenstein, I argue that his work as well as that of various contemporary analytic philosophers provides an alternative to both modernity and constructionism that points toward another version of the settlement.

The third settlement involves a reinterpretation of postmodernism. Although postmodernism has been associated with the worst excesses of linguistic constructionism, it is possible to read the work of certain postmoderns in a very different light. The work of Deleuze and, particularly, Foucault, can be interpreted as accomplishing precisely what postmodernism claimed but generally failed to do: a deconstruction of the discourse/reality dichotomy. Finally, a fourth settlement is emerging in feminist thought. I consider the feminist settlement last in order to highlight its comprehension and scope. My argument is that the feminist settlement is particularly significant in that it provides the clearest articulation of the elements of the new settlement.

I conclude with a discussion of the concept that, I argue, best describes the knowledge/reality connection analyzed in the settlements: disclosure. My argument is that disclosure opens up a space between construction and representation that the settlements are seeking to articulate. Finally, I explore what I call "social ontology." The settlements I discuss are focused primarily on the interface between nature and the discursive and how this interface constitutes knowledge. What is missing from most of these analyses is an account of the social—how social institutions are constituted by the interface of the discursive, the material, the natural, and the technological; how institutions such as politics, economics, and kinship evolve. Turning to Marx, I construct a social ontology that begins to explain this constitution.

My intention here is not to provide an exhaustive survey of contemporary reactions to what Latour calls the failure of the modernist settlement. Rather, it is to selectively discuss the work of theorists who are moving the discussion ahead in useful ways and to contribute to that discussion. I believe that it is imperative that we arrive at a new understanding of the complex relationship among the elements that constitute our world. The purpose of this book is to make a contribution to that new understanding.

1

THE FIRST SETTLEMENT

Philosophy of Science

It should not be necessary to emphasize the centrality of science to the modernist worldview. Science gives us our truth; it is the baseline in a world lacking foundations. Now that God is dead, all we have left is science. Thus if we are going to challenge the modernist settlement that has enthroned science as the sole source of truth, it is necessary to articulate a radically different conception of science. The principal concern of philosophers of science in the modern era has been to define the relationship between science and truth. This concern has also been central to feminist thought. It has been obvious to feminists since the beginning of the modern feminist movement that science is a central element in the constitution of "woman." Questions about women's nature, so basic to the status of women in society, cannot be resolved without reference to science. Thus feminists have always understood that we need a feminist understanding of science if we are to counter the subordination of women.

Twentieth-century philosophy of science has been characterized by a sequence of revolutionary theories. First, of course, there was Thomas Kuhn's *The Structure of Scientific Revolutions* (1962). Although it would be unfair to say that all philosophers of science have embraced Kuhn's theory, it is fair to say that nothing has been the same in the philosophy of science since Kuhn's work. In hindsight, it is clear that Kuhn's book constituted the first step in the linguistic turn that would define the philosophy of science for the rest of the century. Although Kuhn's turn to the linguistic, to the discourse of science rather than the "reality" scientists study, was reluctant, it was nonetheless definitive. Kuhn's argument that the scientists' concepts create the reality that they study seemed, to at least some philosophers of science, irrefutable. It generated a movement among philosophers of science characterized by the embrace of linguistic constructionism at the expense of reality. Another legacy of Kuhn's revolution was equally significant: limiting philosophers of science to two, and only two, possible options with regard to truth—correspondence or coherence. It will become clear in subsequent discussions that reducing our options to one of these two alternatives creates an impossible dilemma for the understanding of scientific truth.

The most notable heirs of Kuhn's theory were those theorists who developed the movement labeled the sociology of scientific knowledge (SSK). Those who espoused SSK studied the work of scientists from a sociological perspective, analyzing how their concepts are constructed and how, in turn, those concepts structure the reality the scientists study. Theorists such as Barry Barnes, David Bloor, and Roy Bhaskar argued that all knowledge, even knowledge in the empirical sciences and mathematics, should be treated as material for investigation. In what came to be called the "strong program in the sociology of knowledge," these theorists argued that science is theoretical knowledge and is thus subject to sociological causation like any other form of knowledge. They attempted to formulate what they called a "post-empiricist" conception of science that, they claimed, entailed epistemological but not ontological relativism (Barnes 1982; Bhaskar 1979).

SSK had a wide-ranging influence on the philosophy of science. The arguments presented by these theorists were, for some, compelling. The detailed studies these theorists produced presented a convincing case for the argument that the concepts that scientists employ are created through a process of social interaction with other scientists. These studies also illustrated that, as Kuhn argued, these concepts create a very specific world for the scientists; they structure the reality the scientist studies. As the concepts change, the reality changes as well. It was hard to deny the logic of these arguments and the claim that science, like any other human action, is a social activity constituted by socially constructed concepts.

But SSK also generated doubts. Some of these doubts centered on what happens in the laboratory. Even if we grant that the scientists' concepts are socially constructed and that these concepts define what counts as reality for the scientist, it is nevertheless the case that something *happens* in the laboratory. Scientists do things with matter, and matter, in turn, does something back. Furthermore, what matter does, how it reacts in the experiment the scientist conducts, determines what the scientist does next. Even within the limited world the scientist has constructed, there are a range of options possible; the result of the experiment is not predetermined. Which of this range of options actually occurs matters for the scientist's practice.

Another set of doubts arose regarding the other entities present in the laboratory: the instruments and technological equipment that the scientist employs. What are we to make of these entities that are not, strictly speaking, natural or human, yet are so central to the practice of science? They are, quite obviously, the scientists' creations. Yet they, like matter, do things. They interact with the scientist and the matter, nature, that he/she studies. The instruments we create in turn create situations that affect the outcome of experiments in the laboratory. They constitute, in short, a unique category: both constructed and material at the same time.

None of these doubts could be accommodated within the parameters of SSK. Philosophers of science consequently began to cast about for an approach that offered an alternative. Several themes emerged in these discussions that would structure the new conception that began to emerge. The first is a movement away from representation. Ian Hacking, for example, argues that the problem with contemporary philosophies of science is their single-minded obsession with representation, thinking, and theory at the expense of intervention, action, and experiment (1983:131). He counters that "the final arbitrator in philosophy is not how we think but what we do" (31). Our theory-dominated history and philosophy of science, he argues, skew our perception of experiment (160). In the process of laboratory science there evolves a tailor-made fit between ideas, our apparatus, and our observation. This is not a coherence theory of truth, Hacking concludes, but a coherence theory of thought, action, materials, and marks (1992:58).[1]

The movement away from representation is central to the evolution of an alternative conception. Since Kuhn, disputes about science have focused on representation and epistemology. What began to emerge in post-Kuhnian discussions, however, was the conviction that an exclusive focus on representation is a dead end. Characterizing the relationship between language and the world in terms of representation provides two equally unacceptable options: coherence or correspondence. Theorists since Kuhn began to argue that what is needed is not a choice between these options but an entirely different approach to the question of knowledge.

As philosophers of science moved away from representation and epistemology, a new issue came into prominence: ontology. The epistemological obsession of much twentieth-century philosophy of science precluded discussions of ontology. Questioning this obsession had the effect of bringing ontology to the forefront of discussions. The work of Isabelle Stengers is a good example of this tendency. Stengers attempts to reformulate Kuhn's approach by arguing that scientific change occurs when nature refuses to express itself in a particular paradigm. Human activity, she argues, "contributes to the production of a new state of nature" (1997:57). Stengers characterizes the relationship of science and nature in terms of "intervention." New scientific ideas are accepted, she argues, because they create a "new mode of the intervention of a phenomenon in discussions between humans" (139). New theories are accepted by scientists because they are interesting—they create active intervention of new associations, new possibilities, new stakes (141).

Another instance of the move from epistemology to ontology is the work of Arthur Fine (1986). Fine elicits Einstein in his effort to articulate a position he calls the Natural Ontological Attitude (NOA). Fine's goal is to save the concept of truth while avoiding the polarity of realism or anti-realism. The significance of the work of theorists such as Stengers and Fine is to shift the emphasis from how we represent nature to how phenomena intervene in human discussions. They argue that theories change, not just because representations change, but because the action of phenomena dictate a change. What is different here is that the phenomena—matter—now have a role in scientific change. They are no longer passive entities constituted by human constructs but players in the game.

Another theme that emerges in the critics of the linguistic turn in the philosophy of science is an emphasis on practice and the laboratories in which scientists engage in that practice. Like the move away from representation, the emphasis on practice exemplifies a movement to a perspective broader than language and representation. The central core of the practice approach is the assertion that practices are embodied, materially mediated arrays of human activity centrally organized around shared practical understandings (Schatzki 2001:2). Like SSK, the practice approach is a social theory. It defines science as a social practice carried out by engaged human actors. But unlike SSK, the practice approach embodies a distinct social ontology: the social is defined as a field of embodied, materially interwoven practices. It is significant that one of the principal architects of SSK, Barry Barnes, has himself embraced the practice approach. He even tries to subsume Kuhn under the practice approach by arguing that Kuhn's paradigms are actually practices (2001:20).

Scientific practices take place in laboratories, and thus those embracing the practice approach have turned their attention to the analysis of laboratories. It is significant that Bruno Latour, the moving force in the articulation of the alternative conception of science that is emerging, first makes his mark with a book on laboratories, *Laboratory Life* (Latour and Woolgar 1986). The analysis of laboratories rather than experiments entails a shift to a perspective beyond discourse. Experimental activity in laboratories, argues Knorr-Certina, occurs in the wider context of equipment and symbolic practices within which the conduct of science is located. The study of laboratories has brought to the fore the full spectrum of activities involved in the production of knowledge. It provides a perspective in which research "intervenes" in both the natural and the social world (1992:115). It also provides a perspective in which ontology is center stage. In *Epistemic Cultures* (1999), Knorr-Certina argues that it is in laboratories that one can see the configuration of several ontologies side by side and investigate their relationship. She concludes that there is an interdependence between ontology and consensus formation in the production of scientific knowledge (1999:253–60).

Perhaps the most concerted effort to formulate an alternative to SSK has come from a group of theorists organized under the label Actor Network Theory (ANT). ANT defines itself very explicitly as opposed to the forms of postmodernism and poststructuralism that are concerned only with language. ANT, its proponents claim, is relational materiality, performativity (Law 1999:4). The purpose of ANT is to assert the principle that entities take their form and acquire attributes as a result of their relations with other entities. ANT rejects the existence of essential, inherent qualities. It also rejects dualisms and instead deconstructs them (1999:3). "Actor Network is, has been, a semiotic machine for waging war on essential differences. It has insisted on the performative character of relations and the objects constituted in these relations" (7).

Several components of ANT are significant for the ongoing discussions in philosophy of science. First, it rejects the postmodern focus on language but not the legitimate insights of the linguistic turn. It recognizes dualisms and seeks to deconstruct them. Second, ANT looks at science from a broader perspective: "ANT is not a theory of the social, any more than it is a theory of the subject or a theory of God, or a theory of nature. It is a theory of the space of fluids circulating in a non-modern situation" (Latour 1999a:22). The result is what one ANT theorist calls "relational materialism" (Law 1994:1). For ANT everything is in flux; there are no clear boundaries. The social is not separated from the natural according to the language/reality dichotomy, but rather they continually interpenetrate each other. Bodies, texts, machines, human and nonhuman entities continually interact in complex relationships.

The New Settlement

The work of Hacking, Fine, and Stengers as well as the adherents of the practice approach and ANT are all important indications of the discontent with the linguistic turn that is spreading throughout the philosophy of science. But there is a certain tentativeness to these accounts. We learn more about what is wrong with social constructionism than what might replace it. What we need at this point, however, is not another critique of social constructionism but a concerted effort to define an alternative approach. Three theorists writing today stand out in that they have succeeded in moving beyond critique to construction. Joseph Rouse, Bruno Latour, and especially Andrew Pickering have begun the difficult task of outlining what Latour calls a "new settlement." Together they provide an understanding of an alternative conception of science that the other critiques have failed to articulate.

In his 1987 book *Knowledge and Power*, Rouse argues: "The world is not something inaccessible on the far side of our theories and observations. It is what shows up in our practices, what resists or accommodates us, as we try to act upon it" (1987:25). This brief statement expresses two related themes that dominate Rouse's approach to the philosophy of science. The first is one other theorists have emphasized: practice. Science, for Rouse and other practice theorists, is an activity that, as he puts it here, shows up in our practices. Scientists *do* things to matter; they are not removed from it in a self-enclosed world of theory.

It is Rouse's second theme, however, that takes his theory beyond the other practice theorists. What is needed in the philosophy of science, Rouse argues, is a turn from representation to manipulation. In order to make his argument, Rouse relies on a reinterpretation of Kuhn. According to Rouse, Kuhn's theory amounts to a deep critique of representationalist epistemology. Rouse reinterprets Kuhn as arguing not that science is a way of representing the world, but that it is a way of manipulating and intervening in it (1987:38). Building on this insight, Rouse argues that we must give up on the dualism of schema and world that is the basis of representationalism. Scientists, he argues, are practitioners not observers; they don't test theories, they use them. The world *is* what shows up in our practices (165).

Rouse's attack on representationalism is even more pronounced in his 1996 book *Engaging Science*. Here he traces the tradition of representationalism back to the classical epistemology of Descartes. What is needed, Rouse argues, is to break with this tradition, to reconceive scientific knowledge on the basis of practice rather than representation. The key to this rethinking is a "narrative" construction of science:

> Understanding scientific practice as narrative reconstruction shows how scientific work becomes coherent and significant without having to rely on problematic notions of scientific community, consensus, or background context. (1996:27)

At the center of Rouse's approach is the argument that representations are not separate from the world; they do not intervene between us and the world. Rather, we have a world that includes sentences, models, images, and their practical and causal interactions with one another (232). Signs signify only by belonging to wide-ranging practices that open up the world as a whole. Practices are what enable the world to display itself as a significant configuration (155). Rouse's anti-representationalism and his emphasis on practices thus merge into a single conception. Scientists are situated knowers engaged in practices. One consequence of this is a rejection of a general theory. One of the problems with representationalism, Rouse argues, is that it is too general. We lose the understanding of science as a specifically local activity and scientists as situated knowers.

One of the significant advantages of Rouse's account is that he does not deny the general thesis of SSK: that the scientist's concepts structure the world that they know. What Rouse wants to do is to incorporate rather than reject this perspective. He argues that it is as much a mistake to reduce science to politics or social construction as it is to restrict it to epistemology (1996:86). Rouse's position is that science is political and it is epistemological, but it is not only these things. He wants to formulate an approach to science that characterizes the actions scientists perform as transforming the situation for further action (66).

Another advantage of Rouse's account is his attention to feminist critiques of science. Rouse argues that there is a distinction between social constructionist and feminist accounts of science on the grounds that, unlike social constructionist accounts, feminist critiques cannot afford to be relativist. Feminist criticism, he asserts, has always remained close to scientific practice (1996:32–33). He chides other philosophers of science for ignoring feminist critiques of science because they do not fit their philosophical perspective (109). Rouse aligns gender studies of science with cultural studies of science as opposed to social constructionist accounts. Cultural/gender studies focus on the emergence of meaning in human practices and avoid the temptation to construct a general theory of knowledge.[2]

Rouse's work takes several significant steps in the direction of the articulation of the new settlement in the philosophy of science. Although his emphasis on practice is exemplary, it is not unique to his theory. What is most valuable in his approach is his discussion of representationalism. Rouse makes it very clear that representationalism is the source of most, if not all, of the problems of the modernist settlement. It can only lead to the dualism of language and reality that is at the root of the dilemma of modernism. By wholly rejecting representationalism, it is possible not only to bring the world back in but to avoid choosing one side of the dualism over the other. But Rouse's work also makes it clear that moving away from representations is a difficult task for contemporary theory. Since at least Descartes, modern thought has been focused on epistemology. Twentieth-century thought in particular has been obsessed with epistemological issues. Moving beyond this obsession is both difficult and necessary.

Rouse's discussion of feminist critiques of science is equally significant. It is revealing both in what it says about his perspective and in what it says about his fellow philosophers of science. As this discussion reveals, few philosophers of science take feminist critiques seriously. Instead, feminist critiques are ghettoized, discussed only by other feminists. In a sense Rouse's interest in feminist critiques is the exception that proves the rule. The exclusion of feminist critiques of science by most philosophers of science, however, is revealing in another sense that Rouse does not discuss. The social constructionists argue that science is a social construction and that its concepts are constitutive of scientific reality. Yet when feminists argue that gender is a major factor in this social construction, most philosophers of science either turn a deaf ear or become very uncomfortable. It is hard to deny that gender is one of the major elements of the social construction of all aspects of human life. Despite this, bringing gender into science seems, even for social constructionists, inappropriate; many find it too extreme. But it is only by bringing gender into science that we will succeed in developing a full understanding of what scientists do.

It should be obvious at this point in the discussion that the key figure in the construction of the new settlement—indeed, the author of the term itself—is Bruno Latour. But Latour's role in the formulation of the new settlement is ambiguous. Latour is, in a sense, the bad boy of the philosophy of science. His early work was influential in establishing the sociology of scientific knowledge as a legitimate field of study. This was no mean feat, given the radical thesis of SSK. At this stage of his career, Latour was adamant in his assertion of what was then a revolutionary notion: the social construction of scientific knowledge and consequently the reality scientists studied. It was evident that Latour relished his stance as the pioneer of this radical theory. It was thus particularly significant when Latour turned on his own theory, repudiating central elements of that theory and moving to a completely different theoretical perspective. But it is also evident that Latour relishes his iconoclastic status today as the author who turns on his own creation.

In 1985 Steven Shapin and Simon Schaffer published a study that is commonly regarded as the first step in the direction of what Latour calls the new settlement. In *Leviathan and the Air Pump*, Shapin and Schaffer examined the relationship between the scientific and political order emerging in seventeenth-century England. They advanced the thesis that solutions to the problem of knowledge are embedded in practical solutions to the problem of social order and that, conversely, different practical solutions to the problem of social order encapsulated contrasting practical solutions to the problem of knowledge (1985:15). On the surface, Shapin and Schaffer's study seems to fall neatly into the tradition of SSK. They are arguing that the scientific triumph of the experimental method that Boyle advocated had its roots in a problem of social order. Experiments were accepted as standard scientific method not because they constituted a superior means of understanding nature but because they solved a problem of social order. What Shapin and Schaffer were arguing and that they demonstrated in the case of seventeenth-century England was that science and politics are inextricably linked. Their most significant point, however, was implicit: that there is nothing wrong with this linkage and that it is normal and expected.

Latour picks up on this theme in his provocative 1993 book *We Have Never Been Modern*. He argues that Hobbes and Boyle are principal architects of what he calls the modernist constitution that defines our era: the separation of nature and culture, science and politics, the human and the nonhuman.[3] But although Latour praises Shapin and Schaffer for their analysis of Hobbes and Boyle, he argues that this analysis does not go far enough. Shapin and Schaffer present Boyle's scientific schema as constructed, but not Hobbes's political schema. What Latour wants to argue is that both discourses are constructed and that they penetrate each other; they are inextricably linked: "Boyle is creating a political discourse from which politics is to be excluded, while Hobbes is imagining a scientific politics from which experimental science has to be excluded" (1993:27).

Latour's principal thesis is that the modernist constitution that Hobbes and Boyle embody entails the separation of science and politics in rhetoric but not in practice. Latour argues that this situation has created an array of fundamental problems for our conception of nature and society as well as our practices. Modernity is rife with paradoxes. Moderns claim that they have not made nature but have made society; then they turn around and claim that they have made nature but not society. Another paradox of the modern constitution that Latour discusses becomes central to the construction of the alternative he is seeking: the creation of hybrids. He argues that "the modern constitution al-

lows the expanded proliferation of hybrids whose existence, whose very possibility, it decries" (1993:34). The modern constitution is rigidly dichotomous. It
allows only for entities that fall on one side or the other of the nature/culture
dichotomy. Hybrids, or cyborgs, don't fit into this schema, and yet the modern
world, unlike any previous era, proliferates the production of hybrids.

Latour concludes: we have never been modern and we have to stop being so
(1993:78). The question, of course, is how? This is the question that occupies Latour first here and then in his subsequent work. Although the outline is sketchy in
this book, a few guidelines emerge. For starters, we must break down the nature/
culture dichotomy. The very notion of culture is an artifact created by bracketing
off the concept of nature. Against this, Latour argues that there is only nature-
culture; no separation is possible (104). Despite their claims to deconstruct
dichotomies, postmoderns are no help here. Postmodernism is parasitic on modernism, caught up in the same dichotomies that imprison modernist thought.
What we need, Latour argues, is

> to retain the production of a nature and of a society that allows changes in size,
> through the creation of an external truth and a subject of law, but without neglect-
> ing the co-production of sciences and societies. (134)

What Latour accomplishes in *We Have Never Been Modern* is not so much
to tell us where we are going as point us in the direction of an alternative conception. One of the strengths of the book is to clarify what is wrong with the
linguistic turn in general and postmodernism in particular. These approaches
err in making discourse independent in the same way that modernity made nature independent. For the postmoderns language is not a mediator between
subject and world but a world unto itself. We need to overcome this error, Latour
argues, before we can move on. Furthermore, he asserts that we need a conception that can accommodate hybrids. Modernism produces hybrids yet denies
their existence. The alternative conception must "give hybrids a new home" by
acknowledging their existence and even granting them agency (1993:51).

Latour introduces the concept of the new settlement and outlines most
clearly what it will look like in *Pandora's Hope* (1999b). His emphasis in this
book is on reality and its loss in the linguistic turn. But the scope of Latour's
argument here goes far beyond the moderns and postmoderns. He traces the
roots of the modernist settlement to the Greeks and their desire to separate
knowledge from the mob. The move to society and social construction, thus,
is a reaction to the separation of objective reality and society that is firmly
rooted in the history of Western thought. But, Latour argues, it is not the right
reaction—it is, rather, a "catastrophe" (1999b:7). What we need, he asserts, is

"a real alternative to that fateful distinction between construction and reality" (16).

Latour begins to define that alternative by offering a replacement for the concept that has caused so many problems in the modernist settlement: "society." His proposal is what he calls the "collective," a concept that refers to the association between humans and nonhumans. "Collective" describes a (political) process by which the cosmos is collected in a livable whole. Its slogan is "no reality with representation" (1999b:304). The collective gives science studies its goal: to tell scientists that the more they are connected to the collective, the better their science will be (18). Our goal, Latour argues, is a "politics of things" (22). Latour's concept of the collective defines an alternative to one of the objects of social constructionism's critique: the correspondence theory of truth. Collectives operate according to "circulating reference," a process that denies an ontological gap between nature and language that we need to bridge (24).

Perhaps the most radical aspect of Latour's settlement is what he calls "articulation." Latour argues for the extension of speech, and specifically the formation of propositions, to nonhumans as well as humans. Referring to his path-breaking study of Pasteur, Latour argues that his analysis of Pasteur's scientific practice reveals that both humans and nonhumans act; both are capable of formulating propositions. This is where articulation comes in: articulation is not a property of speech but a common property of propositions in which many kinds of entities can participate. It follows that articulation is not a property of human speech but an ontological property of the universe (1999b:142). "We speak *because* the propositions of the world are themselves articulated, not the other way around. More exactly, *we are allowed to speak interestingly by what we allow to speak interestingly*" (144). Latour's aim is to move from a vocabulary of subject and object, gap and correspondence to humans and nonhumans, difference, articulation, and propositions (147).[4]

If this all sounds convoluted and unnecessarily complicated, it is because it is. At one point Latour concedes that the new settlement he is seeking is still "cloaked in darkness" (1999b:81). But there are good reasons for this darkness. The strength of the modernist settlement, and consequently the postmodern reaction to it, is pervasive. It will not be easily dislodged. Furthermore, the task that the new settlement must accomplish is daunting. It must carefully thread its way between construction and reality without falling into the errors of choosing either side of the dichotomy to the exclusion of the other. As Latour puts it at one point, "Society is constructed, but not socially constructed" (198). Finally, the new settlement has to incorporate an idea that seems on the face of it counterintuitive: that nonhumans act. Collectives are assemblages of humans and nonhumans, nature and culture, science and politics, and all the elements of the mix act in conjunction with all the other elements. Given our modernist/ postmodernist prejudices, this is a difficult concept to swallow.

> To convince the critically minded that constructionism means access to objectivity, morality, civil peace and piety would require such a deep alteration in our critical ecology it is hard to see how it would come about. (Latour 2003:42)

But of course this "deep alteration" is precisely what Latour is after. The slogan he adopts for his new settlement is "The more constructed the more real" (2003:33).[5] What is important about Latour's work is not so much that he offers a clear description of the outlines of the new settlement. I think it is fair to say that he has not done this. Clarity is not his strong suit. Rather, what Latour has accomplished is to unsettle the assumptions that hold the modernist settlement in place and give it its lasting strength. By being the bad boy of science studies, Latour brings to the forefront what is at stake in the attempt to formulate the new settlement.[6]

That Latour is the major figure in the effort to define an alternative to the modernist settlement, and specifically an approach that avoids the errors of the linguistic turn, is beyond question. Latour's polemical and provocative works have brought the problem to the attention of the academic community more than have those of any other theorist. The very concept of the new settlement is his. But Latour's polemics sometimes stand in the way of his definition of an alternative conception. His desire to shock seems to overcome his desire to clarify. As a result, the parameters of the new settlement that emerge from Latour's work are vague. The diagrams and intersecting circles that are interspersed throughout his work with the aim of defining his conception produce confusion rather than clarity.

Mangle Realism

Another contemporary philosopher of science, however, has succeeded in defining the new settlement with a precision that has eluded its original author. Andrew Pickering offers a definition of this alternative approach that captures the essential features of the new settlement and yet, unlike that of Latour, is clear and compelling. Although Pickering is undoubtedly indebted to Latour, his work represents an advance over the work of Latour because it fills in the gaps in Latour's work and provides an image of the operation of the new settlement.

Pickering's first book, *Constructing Quarks* (1984), emphasized the constitutive force of scientific practice. But like Latour, Pickering ultimately found this perspective too limiting and moved into new theoretical territory in his next book, *The Mangle of Practice* (1995). Pickering begins the book with one of the most controversial aspects of Latour's theory: material agency. The world, Pickering argues, is filled with agency; it is continually doing things that bear on us not as observational statements on disembodied intellects but as forces upon material beings. He also makes the point that much of our everyday life is involved with coping with this material agency, agency that comes from outside the human realm and cannot be reduced to anything within that realm. A useful way of thinking about science, Pickering argues, is an extension and continuation of that coping with material agency. Scientists, as human agents, maneuver in a field of material agency, constructing machines that materialize that agency (1995:6–7).

Pickering's goal is to define what he calls a "performative" image of science, an idiom that subverts the distinctions between human and nonhuman. This "posthumanist space" is

> a space in which the human actors are still there, but now inextricably entangled with the non-human, no longer at the center of the action and calling the shots. The world makes us in one and the same process in which we make the world. (1995:26)

One of the central elements of Pickering's theory is a concept that is conspicuously missing in SSK accounts: resistance. While it is undoubtedly the case that scientists, their concepts, and their instruments structure the experiments that are conducted in laboratories, it is also the case that something *happens* in experiments. Sometimes experiments go according to the scientists' expectations and sometimes they do not. When they don't, when matter resists, then scientists must deal with this resistance and adjust their concepts accordingly. In other words, nature "punches back," and scientists must deal with these punches.

Pickering characterizes the entanglement of the human and the nonhuman as well as the resistances that scientists encounter with a powerful metaphor: the mangle. The mangle is scientific practice: it pulls material agency into the terrain of human agency and structures the goals of human agency (1995:58). What Pickering is trying to depict with his concept of the mangle has much in common with Actor Network Theory. Science, technology and society exist in a field of human and nonhuman agency. Human and nonhuman agents are associated in networks and evolve together in those networks (11). Pickering's concept of the mangle, however, captures the entanglements of the actors in this process in a way that is missing in ANT. The mangle gives us an image for understanding the interaction of the complex elements that constitute scientific practice. It helps us comprehend what these elements are and how they interact more effectively than previous conceptions.

One of the significant advances of the concept of the mangle is what Pickering calls its "impurity" (1995:95). Mangles mix everything up. Diverse elements are thrown into the mangle, and as a result, diverse results emerge. Diversity is missing from SSK accounts of scientific practice, which depict scientific practice as homogeneous: uniform scientific concepts create the uniform material world that scientists study. This uniformity is a product of Kuhn's paradigms that portray the scientific world in lockstep around the agreements that constitute paradigms. Pickering's mangle is much messier. As he puts it, the elements of the mangle "contaminate" each other (95). The action is not determined solely by the scientists' concepts, but rather by the variable mix of elements that interact in the mangle.

Pickering concludes:

> We should see empirical scientific knowledge as constituted and brought into relation with theory via representational chains linking multiple layers of conceptual culture, terminating in the heterogeneous realm of captures and framings of material agency, and sustaining and sustained by another heterogeneous realm, that of disciplined human practices and performances. (111)

In order to make the contrast to SSK even more specific, Pickering goes on to assert that the outcomes of scientific practice depend on "how the world is": "*How the material world is* leaks into and infects our representations of it in a nontrivial and consequential fashion" (183). The result is what he calls "mangle realism," a position distinct from either correspondence or coherence theories of truth.

In a theoretical sense, Pickering is not saying anything that Latour has not expressed. Furthermore, it is important to acknowledge that Latour is the pioneer in the formation of the new settlement. What is important about Pickering, however, is the clarity and force of his conception. Latour has a tendency to dissolve into barely comprehensible discussions studded with intersecting diagrams. He does not provide a clear understanding of what scientific practice would look like under the new settlement. Pickering's mangle, in contrast, offers an image of what is entailed by this new conception. The mangle provides a way of understanding scientific practice that is comprehensible and compelling.

There are four distinct advantages to Pickering's mangle that I will build on in the following discussion. First, Pickering's mangle does not repudiate the insights of the linguistic turn. In the mangle, scientists' concepts *are* constitutive; without them scientists would not be able to access the reality they study.

The error of the linguistic turn was not this insight but rather the assumption that discourse alone is constitutive. The mangle corrects this error. It asserts that scientists' concepts are constitutive, but they are only part of the mix—the mangle—that produces our understanding of reality in both science and everyday life.

The second advantage is the deconstruction of the human/nonhuman dichotomy. The central aspect of this deconstruction is the description of material agency described in the mangle. This is a difficult concept to grasp. It is not an element of either modernity or postmodernism and is, at the very least, unsettling. But Pickering points out that we talk about nonhuman agency all the time in everyday life. We assume, without much reflection, that matter acts on our lives. What the mangle does is incorporate this concept into scientific theory and practice. Matter acts both in the laboratory and in everyday life. The mangle offers an explanation of how this happens and how the agency of matter is intertwined with human agency.

Another aspect of this deconstruction is that the mangle incorporates machines and technology. Since Boyle's air pump, machines in the laboratory have played a key role in the practice of science. Although they are human creations, these machines, like humans and matter, also act. They structure the outcomes of experiments; they act as intermediaries between humans and matter. But they are intermediaries that play a key role in the creation of scientific reality. They occupy a unique position in the pantheon of human and nonhuman entities. To ignore this role is to misunderstand scientific practice in a fundamental way. The mangle incorporates and explicates this key element of scientific practice.

The third advantage of the mangle is that it includes the political/social context of science as an integral and unavoidable element of scientific practice. The mangle acknowledges and accepts that science exists in a political/social context and that politics exist in a scientific context. This interaction and interpenetration is not an aberration or distortion but rather the way things are, the way the world is. The mangle teaches us that we should not be appalled that politics and science are inseparable but should incorporate this interaction into our understanding of the world. The separation of science and politics that was the center of the modernist settlement was an illusion. We need to recognize it as such and develop an alternative conception that presumes their interpenetration.

The fourth advantage of the mangle is its overall effect: the focus of the mangle is the interaction of the constitutive elements. Science, its theory and practice, nature, machines, technology, and politics all interact in the mangle. *Mangle* is both a noun and a verb. It is the entity in which the interaction takes place, but it is also the action that occurs. The elements of the mangle are mangled; they are mixed up with each other into a combination in which the various elements lose their clear boundaries. The mangle teaches us that rather than being shocked by this mix we should accept it and seek to understand it.

Overall, then, what the mangle gives us is an image of how we are located in the world and how the elements of that world interact. In short, it is easy to imagine being *in* the mangle. Pickering conceived of the mangle as a way to explain scientific practice. Scientists are in a mangle when they do their work. Scientific concepts and practice, technology and machines, as well as social and political factors constitute the mangle of scientific practice. But the significant advantage of the mangle is that the metaphor explains more than just science. It illuminates the situation of human agents in the contemporary world in nearly every aspect of our existence. Science, politics, technology, and matter are elements that impinge on almost everything we do. Having a concept that explains their interaction is a significant theoretical advance.

Instances of the mangle range from the most trivial aspects of our lives to the most significant. When I drive to work in my car (or, significantly, my SUV) I am in a mangle constituted by social, political, technological, biological, global, and a host of other elements. Whenever I enter the world of medicine I am in the mangle, a complex of factors constituted by medical knowledge, technology, politics, and social forces. Furthermore, using the concept of the mangle to examine significant political issues is particularly useful. Global warming, for example, is a complicated mangle in which scientific, political, social, and technological factors interact in complex ways. Why is there a right and a left scientific view of global warming? How do we, particularly as non-scientists, assess these views? Did global warming make Katrina more powerful? What is the agentic force here, human or nonhuman or both? The mangle allows us to assess and begin to understand the array of causal factors involved in this and other events.[7]

The mangle is particularly useful in examining the situation of women in the modern world. Unlike men, women have never been allowed to jettison the body and the biological; they have not been allowed to become the disembodied knowers of the Cartesian tradition. Women *are* their bodies, and this association has had a profound effect on the status of women in modernity. Even though the conceptual apparatus of "woman" is constitutive in many ways, it has never been definitive. Women have bodies, and most significantly, they have bodies that reproduce. The linguistic, social, political, and biological are inseparable in the constitution of women in modernity.

The mangle allows us to effectively analyze this constitution. Feminists have gained much from the conceptual analysis of "woman." But much more is involved in this mangle than the linguistic. Women's reproductive function brings science, medicine, and technology into the mangle. Medical technology has transformed reproduction into a highly sophisticated process in which the woman's pregnant body is the subject of extensive medical knowledge. Political factors are paramount as well: laws govern abortion and contraception. But none of these factors are independent. Medical technology allows us to "see" the fetus at earlier and earlier stages. This impinges on the laws governing abortion and the ethics of abortion practices.[8] The advantage of looking at this from the perspective of the mangle is that it allows us to see the interaction and, most importantly, to accept it as the way the world is. In other words, it allows us to stop expecting to separate the elements of the mangle and find the "right" answer. The right answer is that we are in the mangle.

I will employ the mangle metaphor frequently in what follows. Although I agree with Pickering that the mangle describes scientific practice, the concept has a much broader application; and for my purposes, this is its greatest virtue. I will argue that the mangle describes every aspect of contemporary life. We are, all of us, every day, in the mangle. It defines what we know and how we know it. Our task is to try to understand this constitution of knowledge. In this effort I will also utilize the insights of Latour, Rouse, and other philosophers of science writing from this perspective. My reason for focusing on the mangle has more to do with the utility of this metaphor than the deficiencies of the other accounts. My thesis is that we must move forward in the attempt to formulate an alternative conception and that we should use any means at our disposal to accomplish this goal.

2

THE SECOND SETTLEMENT

Analytic Philosophy

> But the world isn't a product. It is just the world.
> —Hilary Putnam

In 1979 Richard Rorty, a philosopher trained in analytic philosophy, issued a broad challenge to the philosophical tradition as a whole. In *Philosophy and the Mirror of Nature,* Rorty argued that what had been the goal of philosophy since its inception must be completely abandoned. Since Plato, philosophy had been defined as the search for universal, absolute truth, truth that transcends culture and history. Since Descartes, this search had been defined more narrowly in terms of the correspondence between language and reality, the effort to mirror nature in our precisely defined concepts. Rorty's thesis is that this search is misguided and that seeking truth, most notably universal truth, is not only an illusion but is counterproductive. What we need now, he asserts, is a new definition of philosophy that has no relation to objectivity and truth, that abandons the search altogether. As an alternative, he proposes an "edifying philosophy," one that does not seek correspondence to reality but rather aims to continue "the conversation of mankind."

It should go without saying that the profession of philosophy did not immediately embrace Rorty's prescription. It should also go without saying that there is no monolithic entity "the philosophical profession" that reacted uniformly to Rorty's prescription. But there is something to be learned about "philosophy" from Rorty's book. For most of the twentieth century, academic philosophy had been divided into two distinct camps: the Anglo-American and the continental. Rorty's book is premised on this distinction. His discussion both entails and perpetuates a set of assumptions that has been widely accepted in both philosophical camps. These assumptions include the characterization of continental philosophy, and particularly the postmodern variant, as relativistic and even nihilistic. The parallel assumption is that Anglo-American analytic philosophy has stubbornly clung to the illusion of truth and objectivity despite the onslaughts of linguistic constructionism. Rorty's examples of "edifying philosophers" are, with the significant exception of Wittgenstein, all continental philosophers.

Although these assumptions apply to some philosophers in each camp, the situation is much more complex than this dichotomy indicates. In this chapter and the next I will argue that these characterizations of the analytic and continental traditions are inaccurate. Some continental philosophers, most notably Foucault and, although I will not discuss him, Gadamer, are very far from being linguistic constructionists. They have brought the material and the ontological into the equation despite their emphasis on the linguistic. A parallel movement can be discerned in the analytic camp. Philosophers such as Putnam, Davidson, and, as I will argue, Wittgenstein develop a position that incorporates the material and the discursive without favoring either side of the dichotomy.

This convergence between the analytic and continental traditions is the subject of Linda Alcoff's significant book *Real Knowing*. "This book," she declares at the outset, "is located within what is, I hope, an emerging paradigm shift in epistemology that might broadly call itself 'social epistemology'" (1996:2). Alcoff's goal is to establish a dialogue between analytic and continental philosophers. Her strategy is to provide an account of knowledge that is self-conscious about the interconnections between knowledge, power, and desire without relinquishing what she sees to be the essential element: that claims to know are claims *about something* (6).

Alcoff's characterization of the position she is both describing and advocating is "ontologically robust coherentism" (1996:6). This position will, she hopes, transcend the binary between nature and human construction. Both analytic and continental philosophers, she argues, are moving toward this coherentist position. Alcoff chooses representatives from both traditions to establish her thesis. Her choices from the continental tradition are Gadamer and Foucault. For Alcoff, Gadamer's perspective is ontological, not epistemological. Gadamer, she claims, offers an ontological argument about the structure of understanding. For Gadamer, understanding is ontologically dependent on an evolving tradition. Unlike the social constructionists, Gadamer defines truth not as constructed but as an event mediated by inquiry. Gadamer's ontology of truth, Alcoff concludes, constitutes an immanent metaphysics (66).

Davidson and Putnam are Alcoff's selections from the analytic tradition. She argues that there is a strong similarity between Gadamer's emphasis on tradition and Davidson's web of belief. Davidson's assertion that we judge the truth or error of beliefs against the background of a web of beliefs that is true closely parallels Gadamer's discussion of prejudice (Alcoff 1996:104). Alcoff aligns Putnam's position with that of Foucault. Like Foucault, Putnam examines the versions of reality that have become dominant. But Putnam goes beyond Foucault to relate these conceptions to human flourishing (1996:217). Alcoff labels the position that she ascribes to these philosophers "immanent realism" (218). An immanent realist view, she claims, allows us to differentiate between true and false claims while still defining truth as historical. The coherentist ontology of truth she is defining does not entail that truth is irrational, subjective, or ideological (229). Rather, it acknowledges the historical situatedness of truth without abandoning the possibility of truth claims.

My search for a "new settlement" is closely related to Alcoff's search for what she calls a new ontological paradigm. I will build on many of her insights in the following discussion. But there are limitations to Alcoff's approach that I will attempt to address in my analysis. First, although Alcoff frequently refers to "ontology" in her work, her point of reference remains epistemological: the title of her book is "Real Knowing," and she argues for a "coherentist" approach. My contention is that remaining within the epistemological framework is counterproductive at this point. We need a clearer break with epistemological questions to move to the new paradigm Alcoff is seeking. The focus on epistemology and representationalism is the origin of the problem we are now facing.

Second, despite her previous feminist work, Alcoff's analysis in *Real Knowing* is not explicitly feminist. Although she makes passing reference to the significance of her work for feminism, it is not the center of her analysis. This is a serious oversight. It is my contention that feminism is central to the new ontological paradigm that is emerging. Feminist thought on nature and the body is essential to the definition of that paradigm. Feminists have been and continue to remain at the forefront of the new settlement. Women were a bad fit in both modernist and postmodernist thought; their search for a new paradigm is a product of that dis-ease. One of the central issues for the new settlement that is emerging will be feminist issues such as the body, reproduction, sexual abuse, and the exploitation of women.

My intent in this chapter and the next, then, is to define and further elaborate on the new settlement that is emerging in contemporary philosophy. Like
Alcoff, I see this settlement emerging in both analytic and continental philosophy. In this chapter I will focus on an analytic philosopher; in the next, on a
continental thinker. In both analyses, however, my emphasis will be on reinterpretation. My thesis is that the dominant interpretation of the work of Wittgenstein and Foucault has been skewed by the concerns of the linguistic turn. We
have been so caught up in the analysis of language that dominated twentieth-
century thought that we interpret every approach in strictly discursive terms.
Against this I am asserting that reading Wittgenstein and Foucault across the issues raised by theorists such as Latour and Pickering produces a very different
understanding of their work. It is an understanding that can move us in the direction of another approach to the relationship between language and reality.

In his analysis of analytic and continental philosophy, Rorty is correct about
one thing: analytic philosophers have never been enamored of linguistic constructionism. This dis-ease has taken different forms. John Searle's perspective on
the issue is particularly trenchant. In *The Construction of Social Reality* (1995)
Searle's thesis is simple and straightforward: "We live in exactly one world, not
two or three or seventeen" (1995:ix). He makes a clear distinction between what
he calls "institutional facts," those dependent on human agreement, and "brute
facts," those that do not require human institutions for their existence. These two
sets of facts interact in specific ways. The statement that the sun is 93 million
miles from the earth requires the institution of language and the institution of
defining distance in miles, but the fact stated exists independent of any institutions (27). This leads Searle to his definition of realism: it is not a theory of truth
but an ontology. On his terms one can espouse external realism and reject the
correspondence theory of truth. Realism does not imply that there is a privileged
vocabulary by which reality can be described. It follows that there is no contradiction between conceptual relativism and external realism (161). At the end of his
book, Searle offers a Wittgensteinian defense of his position: "I have not shown
that there is a real world but only that you are committed to its existence when
you talk to me or anyone else" (194).

Searle's position is obviously very much his own. Other contemporary analytic philosophers approach the issue in equally distinctive ways. The spirit of
Searle's account, however, is widely shared. As Hilary Putnam puts it so suc-
cinctly, "The world isn't a product" (1990:28). Putnam's "internal realism," like
Searle's "external realism," is an effort to retain what we all know, that we live
in one world, while at the same time acknowledging that we can only access that
world through language. As Donald Davidson puts it, "In giving up the dualism
of scheme and world we do not give up the world, but re-establish unmediated

touch with familiar objects whose antics make our sentences and opinions true or false" (2001:198). Like the philosophers of science discussed in chapter 1, Davidson wants to bring the world back in by emphasizing the obvious: that we presuppose the existence of that world in everyday life.

In my exploration of the new settlement that is emerging in analytic philosophy I could, like Alcoff, pursue the work of Davidson, Putnam, Searle, or another contemporary philosopher. But I am adopting a more radical strategy. My thesis is that a better grounding for the new settlement can be found in the work of the philosopher whose approach is the foundation of many of the analytic philosophers' discussions of these issues: Ludwig Wittgenstein. Wittgenstein occupies a curious position in this discussion. On one hand, he is commonly seen as the father of analytic philosophy, a tradition that has repudiated linguistic constructionism. On the other hand, however, Wittgenstein is also closely associated with the linguistic turn in philosophy and is indeed identified as one of its key architects. Rorty places him in his category of "edifying philosophers." I will exploit this ambiguity in the following analysis. My thesis is that it was not Wittgenstein's intention to divorce the discursive and the material, to embrace either realism or anti-realism. Although Wittgenstein is without doubt deeply, almost exclusively, concerned with language, he is neither the linguistic constructionist that some of his interpreters have made him out to be nor the realist of other interpretations.

My focus on Wittgenstein offers several advantages for my project. First, as one of if not the most prominent philosophers of the twentieth century, his work can provide a solid grounding for the position I am advocating here. If Wittgenstein can be shown to be, in Karen Barad's terminology, an intra-actionist, the position gains an important defense. Second, if it can be shown that the alleged architect of the linguistic turn is, in fact, advocating a position that repudiates linguistic constructionism, it puts this position in a very different light. Latour claims that we have never been modern. Maybe we can turn his theory around and claim that we have never been linguistic constructionists either. If the purported founder of linguistic constructionism is not, in fact, advocating that position, then it calls for a reassessment of the movement itself.

Wittgenstein's Settlement

A picture held us captive. And we could not get outside it, for it lay in our language and language seemed to repeat it to us inexorably. (1958:§48)

Many of Wittgenstein's comments on philosophy are about breaking free— breaking free from the picture that held us captive, letting the fly out of the fly bottle, halting our desire for endless explanation. On the surface, these references seem quite straightforward, but as with any aspect of Wittgenstein's philosophy, this is not the case. The first question, of course, is what we are breaking free *from*. For Wittgenstein it does seem clear that this is the error of the philosophical view he is repudiating. This view, significantly, is itself a picture theory, the picture theory of language and its relationship to reality. It is also clear that Wittgenstein himself embraced this theory in his early work, asserting that statements must accurately mirror the reality they describe. But once we move beyond these points, things become less obvious. In *Philosophy and the Mirror of Nature* Rorty argues that if we reject the picture theory we must move to embrace a form of linguistic constructionism that eschews any connection to reality. For Rorty, thus, rejecting modernity entails a form of postmodernism or, at the very least, social construction. But is Rorty stacking the deck here? Is this the only option? Does rejecting the picture theory of language necessarily lead to a rejection of any discussion of reality or of the material world?

These are important questions for approaching Wittgenstein's later philosophy. Wittgenstein is not Rorty. He is writing at a time when the kind of linguistic constructionism that Rorty embraced was not on the philosophical agenda. We need not assume, thus, that Wittgenstein, in rejecting this picture—that is, the picture theory of language—embraced a position that entails the linguistic construction of reality. Wittgenstein wanted to correct the errors of the picture theory, but it does not follow that he wanted to erect a barrier between language and reality. His goal was to explain the relationship between language and reality in a way that avoided the errors of the picture theory.

What I am arguing, then, is that Wittgenstein's position is a complex one that provides an understanding of the interrelationship between the discursive and the material distinct from linguistic constructionism. His discussion of language games as activities, of general facts of nature, form of life, and many other concepts suggests an interactive understanding of the relationship between the discursive and the material. It suggests an understanding close to the practice theorists discussed in chapter 1. Perhaps because Wittgenstein began with the picture theory, he could never entirely divorce himself from a connection to reality. He believed that he got it wrong the first time but that the solution was not to ignore reality entirely. Rather, it was to incorporate the discursive and the material in a more complex way.

The interpretation of Wittgenstein I am offering here is not, of course, unique. Many commentators have remarked on his "realism" and his assertion of the grounding of our concepts in the "natural" world. What I am claiming, however, is that interpreting Wittgenstein's work from the perspective of the issues raised by theorists such as Pickering and Latour is valuable in several respects. Wittgenstein's work has frequently been used to support the linguistic constructionist position. If this can be shown to be false, these supports fall away and with it the plausibility of the position. But more importantly, if I can show an affinity between Wittgenstein's work and the interactionist theory emerging today, it can significantly bolster that theory. I am reinterpreting Wittgenstein, in short, to help define and promote the new settlement in contemporary thought.

In retrospect it is tempting to interpret Wittgenstein's *Tractatus* as an indictment of logical positivism rather than its most concise description. The *Tractatus* is about propositions and how they must be accurately framed. But it is not difficult to discern an underlying dissatisfaction with the account. Wittgenstein begins with his now famous statement that "what can be said at all can be said clearly, and what we cannot talk about we must pass over in silence" (1961:3). He then goes on:

> Thus the aim of the book is to set a limit to thought, or rather—not to thought but to the expression of thought: for in order to be able to set a limit to thought, we should have to find both sides of the limit thinkable (i.e., we should have to be able to think what cannot be thought).
>
> It will therefore only be in language that the limit can be set, and what lies on the other side of the limit will simply be nonsense. (3)

Several pages later he asserts that he has found the solution to the problems he set forth, but that the value of the work is to demonstrate how little is achieved when these problems are solved (5). Finally, he concludes the book with the statement with which he began: what we cannot speak about we must pass over in silence (151).

Clearly, something is wrong here, even in Wittgenstein's eyes. He has said all he can about propositions and their truth, but it is not satisfactory. The limits of the world as he has described it are too restrictive. There are too many things that must be passed over in silence. What he appears to conclude in his later work is that instead of focusing on propositions he should have focused on language. Language, he argues later, is an activity. It is something human beings do. It is central to their form of life. The abstraction of propositions is the problem. Cutting them off from human activity not only limits our world but creates a false division between language and the world.

Wittgenstein's perception that the error of his discussion of propositions was their abstraction sets the stage for his later discussion of language. The presumption informing Wittgenstein's discussion of language in this work is that language is an activity and, most notably, an activity that is at the center of the human form of life. When discussing language, Wittgenstein does not make the same error that he made in his discussion of propositions—abstraction from the activity of everyday life. Wittgenstein's discussion of language is grounded, contextual, rooted in the practices that constitute human life.

At the center of Wittgenstein's discussion of language is, of course, his unique concept: the language game. Discussions of language games, examples of languages, are scattered throughout Wittgenstein's later philosophy. In *Philosophical Investigations* he offers a very straightforward definition of the concept: "Here the term 'language-game' is meant to bring into prominence the fact that the *speaking* of language is part of our activity, of a form of life" (1958:§23). "And to imagine a language is to imagine a form of life" (§19). Language games, we are told, are multiple; if we don't keep the multiplicity of language games in view, we will tend to ask misleading questions (§24).

From the outset, Wittgenstein wants to make it clear that he is not offering a comprehensive, universal theory of language. That was the problem with the "picture" that he is trying to overcome. The choice of "game" to discuss language is thus significant. There is nothing common to all games; they have similarities, family resemblances; they form a family (1958:§67). But it is impossible to define the "essence" of a game. Thus, "instead of producing something common to all we call language, I am saying these phenomena have no one thing in common which makes us use the same word for all—but that they are *related* to each other in many different ways" (§65). Wittgenstein keeps coming back to two themes: the complexity and multiplicity of language games, and their relation to human activity. "Language, I should like to say, relates to a *way* of living," and "In order to describe the phenomenon of language, one must describe a practice, not something that happens once, no matter of what kind" (1978:335). Language is an instrument; it allows us to do the multitude of things that we do as human beings. "Concepts lead us to make investigations; are the expression of our interest, and direct our interest" (1958:§570).

In the end, then, "Language is just a phenomenon of human life" (1978:351). The examination of language games gets its importance from the fact that language games continue to function (1978:208). Although in some sense this sounds too simplistic, it is the principal point that Wittgenstein is pressing. His argument is that too much of philosophy has been concerned with complicated universal theories of language and its relationship to the world. Wittgenstein wants to replace all this with a simple maxim: language is something we *do* as human beings. Its uses are multiple because human beings engage in various and diverse activities. But ultimately these activities can all be described through the examination of language games because of the intimate relationship between language and human life.[1]

A significant aspect of Wittgenstein's discussion of language games is his examination of "primitive language games." His claim is not that all language games are primitive but rather that analyzing primitive language games will help us to understand the functioning of other, less primitive language games. One of Wittgenstein's examples of a "primitive language," a builder and his assistant (1958:§2), has been extensively analyzed by his critics. The point of this example is that, as with all language games, what is involved is an *activity*. The builder and his assistant are doing something—building a building—and language is an integral part of that activity. The builder and his assistant have tools *and* language, which is itself a tool.

Closely related to Wittgenstein's discussion of primitive language games is his assertion that children are taught their native language by means of language games (1960:81). Learning language is something human beings do and something that we, unlike other creatures, *can* do. You can teach a dog to retrieve, but not a cat (90). Teaching a child a primitive language game, Wittgenstein asserts, is training not explanation (1958:§5). But Wittgenstein wants to go even deeper into human nature than the claim that language and human nature are inextricably connected. He also wants to claim that in some cases primitive language games are "reactions," that they have pre-linguistic roots. It is a primitive reaction to tend and treat someone who is in pain. "Primitive" here means "pre-linguistic." A language game is based on primitive reaction, but it does not have its root in thought (1970:95). Although Wittgenstein does not spell out the implications of this argument, it seems to blur the distinction between the linguistic and the nonlinguistic activities of human beings. It seems to follow that privileging language in human activity is inappropriate, a tendency to which philosophers are particularly prone.

In all of these discussions Wittgenstein never loses sight of the goal of his investigations: to correct philosophical confusions. If we want to study truth and falsehood, agreement of propositions with reality, and so on, we should look at primitive forms of language, which do not have the confusing background of highly complicated processes of thought. We can then build more complicated forms on the primitive forms (1960:17). One of the principal advantages of the study of primitive languages is that it allows us to understand the relationship between words and meaning. "Only in the practice of a language can a word have meaning" (1978:344). And, more pointedly, "The concept of meaning I adopt in my philosophical discussions originates in a primitive form of language" (1974:56). Meaning and understanding, Wittgenstein argues, are always embedded in language games. Understanding entails knowing how to *use* a word. It is not a process that accompanies reading or hearing but an interrelated process against a background and in a context. That context is the actual use of a learned language (74). Certain kinds of understanding, he asserts, are even tied to human nature—like pointing a finger to explain something (94).

Wittgenstein brings this together in his now famous statement in the *Philosophical Investigations*: "For a *large* class of cases—though not for all—in which we apply the word 'meaning' it can be defined thus: the meaning of a word is its use in the language" (1958:§43). Wittgenstein's goal here, as it so often is, is to combat the erroneous view that meaning is a mental activity added onto the speaking or writing of a word. He also wants to reject the notion that there is *one* relation of a name to its object and our goal is to find this one correct relationship (1960:173). But it is important to note that he is not replacing this view with a version of coherentism. He is not defining meaning as internal to language, solely a product of discourse. Rather, he is defining meaning as a product of our *activity* as human beings engaged in language games. Meaning is tied to use, to something we do. He even asserts that it is in some cases tied to our human nature. Meaning is connected to our reality as human beings and a product of human activity. It is not a mental event, but it is also not a purely linguistic construction.[2]

Commentators on Wittgenstein's later philosophy have devoted much attention to his discussion of rules. This aspect of Wittgenstein's thought is not directly relevant to my discussion here. However, I would like to emphasize one aspect of Wittgenstein's discussion of rules that reinforces the interpretation I am advancing. In *Remarks on the Foundation of Mathematics* Wittgenstein asserts: "Following the rule is a human activity" (1978:331). This entails that "to obey a rule, [to] make a report, to give an order, to play a game of chess, are *customs* (uses, institutions)" (1958:§199). Rules are practices that are taught; they involve training. Rules cannot be described in general because they are a product of training, not description (1970:59). Rules, like meaning, are not singular but multiple. "Our rules leave loop-holes open, and the practice has to speak for itself" (1969:21). The conclusion here, as with language games in general, is to emphasize what we do. Discussions of rules have a tendency to get lost in philosophical speculation about precise definitions. Wittgenstein wants to avoid this error.

One of the notable aspects of Wittgenstein's later philosophy is his discussion of a number of issues that suggest a connection between language games and nature: the nature of human beings and their form of life, the nature of the material world in which we live, our natural history. Wittgenstein scholars have been very interested in these comments, and much has been written about them. It is not my intent here to survey that literature or to refute or endorse the positions taken in it. This aspect of Wittgenstein's thought, however, is central to my interpretation of his position. I will argue that these comments indicate that Wittgenstein is trying to define a distinctive relationship between language and the material world, the natural world as well as the parameters of human existence. It is an understanding that departs from the realism of the picture theory. But it is also an understanding that does not neatly conform to linguistic constructionism. My argument is that Wittgenstein's position here describes a complex interaction between language and reality that accounts for the central role that each plays in our understanding. It is also a position that has much in common with the interactionist position emerging today.

One of the indications that Wittgenstein is articulating a position far from linguistic constructionism is his discussion of two issues that are highly problematic for this position: color and mathematics. Neither of these issues fits into the understanding of the world posed by linguistic constructionism. Color seems to suggest a primordial sensation that, although described by language, is not encompassed by it. Mathematics, likewise, seems to be connected to the "real" world in a unique way. Although undoubtedly a human invention, it seems to necessitate a connection to the material world that transcends its human origins.

In *Remarks on Color* (1977) Wittgenstein begins by asking us to imagine a tribe of colorblind people. Their color concepts, he asserts, would be different from ours. The normally sighted and the colorblind do not have the same concept of colorblindness. A colorblind person cannot learn the use of color concepts; nor can he/she learn to use the word *colorblind* as a normal person does. One of the points that Wittgenstein makes in his discussion is that color concepts operate differently and are in a different relation to each other. Some color concepts can be described as transparent or deeper or darker, others cannot.

These remarks do not lead to an obvious conclusion either that the reality of the world dictates our concepts or that our concepts create a (colored) reality. Rather, they suggest that the relationship is complex, not subject to a simple formula. Wittgenstein offers various versions of his position in different contexts. On one hand, he asserts, "I couldn't think that something is red if red didn't exist" (1974:143). He also argues that if human beings were not in general agreed about the color of things then our concept of color would not exist (1970:64). Finally, he declares what is obvious: we have a color system, and we have a number system. Then he asks: Do the systems reside in *our* nature or in the nature of things? Instead of answering this question, he asks another: "Is there something arbitrary about this system?" When he finally answers these questions, his reply is ambiguous: "Yes and no. It is akin both to what is arbitrary and to what is non-arbitrary" (1970:65–66).

It is hard to know what to make of this passage except that the relationship between language and reality in these particular cases is especially complex.

This relationship, he concludes, is both arbitrary and not. It is arbitrary in the sense that concepts are conventional—they vary from language to language. But the relationship is not arbitrary in the sense that, as Wittgenstein explains in the case of color, we would not have a concept of red if there were not red things in the world. This understanding of the complicated relationship between language and reality emerges in other aspects of Wittgenstein's work. In *Philosophical Investigations* he discusses the practice of weighing. The practice of weighing a piece of cheese, for example, would lose its point if cheese frequently changed in size and weight for no reason (1958:§142). The fact that cheese does not act this way grounds our language game. In *On Certainty* he states, "If we imagine the facts otherwise than as they are, certain language-games lose some of their importance, while others become important" (1969:10).

A central aspect of Wittgenstein's understanding of the complex relationship between concepts and reality is his discussion of "natural history." In *Philosophical Investigations* he states: "What we are supplying are really remarks on the natural history of human beings; we are not contributing curiosities however, but observations which no one has doubted, but which have escaped remark only because they are always before our eyes" (1958:§415). And he writes, "Commanding, questioning, recounting, chatting are as much a part of our natural history as walking, eating, drinking, playing" (§25). This "natural history" even extends to logic: "What you say seems to amount to this, that logic belongs to the natural history of man" (1978:352). Pain behavior may also fall into this category (1970:96).

These references suggest several interpretations. One way of reading them is that there are certain basic facts about human life and the material world in which we live—that pieces of cheese do not arbitrarily change weight, for example—that determine the concepts we employ. If these facts were to change, our concepts would have to change as well. Although this is a plausible interpretation, I think Wittgenstein is suggesting a more complicated relationship here. He is rejecting a one-to-one correspondence between concepts and reality and suggesting instead a complex interaction between the two that is not deterministic in any sense. It is just such a one-to-one correspondence that he is rejecting in the picture theory. In *Remarks on Color* he asks, "Would it be correct to say our concepts reflect our life?" An affirmative answer to this question would be consistent with the above interpretation. But that is not Wittgenstein's answer. Instead he states, "They stand in the middle of it" (1977:57). This statement indicates that the position Wittgenstein is taking here is an interactionist one that, I assert, has much in common with that described by theorists such as Pickering and Latour. Concepts and reality are intertwined. Neither one determines the other. We are always in the middle of things—in the mangle, in Pickering's sense—in that our world is defined both by our concepts and by the material reality they describe. Our world *is* the intersection and inter-twining of both. Deborah Orr captures the sense of this intersection when she argues that for Wittgenstein the body and lived experience are "the weft into which language is woven to create the pattern of our lives" (2002:323).

Wittgenstein summarizes his position here in this famous passage from *Philosophical Investigations:*

> I am not saying: if such and such facts of nature were different people would have different concepts (in the sense of a hypothesis). But: if anyone believes that cer-tain concepts are absolutely the correct ones, and that having different ones would mean not realizing something we realize, then let him imagine certain very gen-eral facts of nature to be different from the ones that we are used to, and the forma-tion of concepts different from the usual ones will become intelligible to him. (1958:IIxii)

Several commentators have suggested that the position Wittgenstein outlines here dissolves the realist/anti-realist distinction that philosophers have so heat-edly disputed (Bloor 1997:xi; Lynch 1992:226; Sewell 2001). I think we can go beyond even this in an assessment of Wittgenstein on this point. Like the theo-rists who are trying to define Latour's "new settlement," Wittgenstein is here not solving the realist/anti-realist debate but suggesting that the terms of the debate are wrongheaded. Language does not constitute reality nor does reality determine language. Both positions are in error, and to understand the interac-tion of these elements we need a new understanding of their relationship.

Central to that new understanding is Wittgenstein's concept of "form of life." This concept has also received much attention from Wittgenstein's critics. Part of the controversy revolves around the same set of issues that inform dis-cussions of natural history: is Wittgenstein arguing for a one-to-one correspon-dence between the natural necessities of human life and our concepts? Witt-genstein's discussion of "form of life," however, has raised another issue: is Wittgenstein a cultural relativist in that he is arguing that each culture has a distinctive form of life that defines reality for that culture? This issue, as New-ton Garver (1990) argues, hinges on whether Wittgenstein uses the concept in the singular or the plural. Garver argues that the proper understanding of "form of life" in Wittgenstein is that human beings have a single form of life that is intimately related to the language games that we practice. Against the majority of commentators, Garver argues that Wittgenstein did not assume a plurality of human forms of life, only a plurality of languages (1990:182).

In *Philosophical Investigations* Wittgenstein states, "It is what human be-ings *say* that is true and false; and they agree in the *language* they use. That is not agreements in opinions but in form of life" (1958:§241), and "What has to be accepted, the given, is—so one could say—*forms of life*" (1958:IIxi). These and other passages can be read to establish, on one hand, that Wittgenstein is a biological determinist, that he is claiming that the natural, biological facts of human life determine how we live as human beings. It can just as plausibly be interpreted, on the other hand, as a statement of cultural relativism, the assertion that the different cultural practices of humans create different forms of life. Against both of these interpretations I would like to suggest another way of reading these passages. What Wittgenstein is doing here is deconstructing the dichotomy between the biological and the cultural. He is claiming on one hand that the human form of life is limited by certain biological facts of human life. As humans, we need food, shelter, cooperation with other humans (O'Grady 2004:332). The question then arises as to whether the differences between various cultures' ways of attaining these biological necessities entail that human beings have multiple forms of life. Or, alternatively, do cultural differences obliterate human universals? What Wittgenstein's perspective leads us to consider is that the best way to approach this issue is not to decide on one or the other of these extremes, but rather to evaluate it in terms of emphasis. We may want to emphasize the differences between human cultures and thus posit multiple forms of life. Or we may want to stress the commonalities among all human communities. In either case Wittgenstein's point is the same: our form(s) of life is constrained by certain facts of human existence. These facts do not determine the language games we practice, but they interact in significant ways with those language games.

Rupert Read (2002) argues that Wittgenstein's concept of form of life entails that we share a pattern of living and a common environment in which the natural and cultural elements are not qualitatively distinguishable. Stanley Cavell puts it somewhat differently: We are creatures for whom custom and convention are our nature (1979:111). Significantly, this is not true of all creatures: "If a lion could talk, we would not understand him" (Wittgenstein 1958:IIxi). Human beings talk; they develop customs and conventions. Lions do not. Central to our form of life is the practice of language games. This practice is tied to our natural history as human beings and the natural facts of human being. Language games vary greatly from culture to culture. But they all are connected in different ways to that natural history.

Once more I am suggesting that Wittgenstein's position can profitably be read across the formulations developed by the theorists I am examining here. Donna Haraway developed the concept of nature/culture to deconstruct this dichotomy. Likewise, Wittgenstein argues that the attempt to sort out which is which, which elements of our life are natural and which cultural, is futile and counterproductive. That was the error of the modernist settlement that Latour exposes. Instead, Wittgenstein is arguing that nature and culture merge in the practices of human beings, in what we *do*, and that a central and unique thing that humans do is to talk. What we have, in effect, is another version of the mangle.

Wittgenstein's discussion of form of life is closely connected to his examination of the issue of certainty. Once more the question is the relationship between language and reality: are our concepts grounded in absolutely certain facts that make them correct, or are they grounded in culturally variable human conventions? Wittgenstein's answer, again, is ambiguous. In *On Certainty* Wittgenstein approaches the question with his famous riverbed analogy. Nothing captures his sense of ambiguity better than this analogy. Riverbeds, like propositions, can seem sometimes to be hardened, sometimes fluid:

> It might be imagined that some propositions, of the form of empirical propositions, were hardened and functioned as channels for such propositions as were not hardened but fluid; and that this relation altered with time, in that fluid propositions hardened, and hard ones became fluid. (1969:15)

The key, Wittgenstein argues, is distinguishing between the movement of the water on the riverbed and the shift of the bed itself. He concludes:

> And the bank of that river consists partly of hard rock, subject to no alteration or only to an imperceptible one, partly of sand, which now in one place now in another gets washed away or deposited. (1969:15)

Wittgenstein's point is that our conviction of certainty is not arbitrary, but neither is it grounded in indubitable facts. It is, as with everything else human beings do, part of a system, a practice. "This system is not so much the point of departure as the elements in which our arguments have their life" (1969:16). The end of this system is not an ungrounded proposition but "an ungrounded way of life" (17). What seems to be certain, what stands fast, does so because it is held fast by what lies around it (21). The difficulty, Wittgenstein asserts, is realizing the groundlessness of our beliefs (24), realizing that justification comes to an end (27). Wittgenstein's point here seems to be that what we have to accept is that things are not as simple as we had hoped. The end of justifications is not, as we might wish, certain propositions that strike us as immediately true, something we can *see*. Rather, giving grounds ends in our *acting*, which is at the bottom of the language game (28). "At the foundation of well-founded belief lies belief that is not founded" (33). Some things have to hold fast—the hinges on the door—in order for our way of life to continue to function.

Even though it is difficult to figure out exactly what Wittgenstein is arguing *for* here, it is clear what he is arguing *against*. The notion that we can find some objective, absolutely certain propositions to ground knowledge is, he claims, a fiction. It is part of the picture theory that is holding us captive. In *Philosophical Investigations* Wittgenstein uses the analogy of slippery ice to describe this mind-set: "We have got on to slippery ice where there is no friction and so in a sense the conditions are ideal, but also just because of that, we are unable to walk. We want to walk: so we need *friction*. Back to the rough ground!" (1958:§107). The preconceived idea of a crystalline purity must be rejected by "turning our whole examination around" (§108). We accomplish this turnaround by focusing on what we *do*, not solely on what we *say*: "Our mistake is to look for an explanation where we ought to look at what happens as a 'proto-phenomenon.' That is, when we ought to have said: *this language game is played*" (§654). And, even more to the point, "If I have exhausted the justifications I have reached bedrock, and my spade is turned. Then I am inclined to say: 'This is simply what I do'" (§217).

One pole in the debate over certainty is the absolutist position—the quest for indubitable truth. It is quite clear that Wittgenstein rejects this pole. It is less clear that he rejects the other pole—the conventional, relativist position that language creates reality. That Wittgenstein has been interpreted as a linguistic relativist is undeniable. But his discussion of certainty offers one of the most significant refutations of this interpretation. Wittgenstein asserts that the ground of our certainty is our practice, what we *do* as human beings, our form of life. This assertion, taken in conjunction with what he says about natural history and general facts of nature, leads to the conclusion that this form of life is not arbitrary. As human beings there are limits and constraints that structure our form of life. To assert that "this is simply what we do" is not to surrender to convention, but rather it is to recognize that human life has limits.

In retrospect it is ironic that one of the examples that Wittgenstein chooses to illustrate the constraints on our form of life is travel to the moon. In Wittgenstein's lifetime travel to the moon seemed a safe example of what lay beyond human possibility. The fact that humans succeeded in going to the moon some twenty years after his death is in a sense irrelevant; the example still supports the point I am making here. We believe, Wittgenstein states, that it is impossible to go to the moon. There may be people who believe it is possible. He then comments: "These people do not know a lot that we know. And, let them be never so sure of their belief—they are wrong and we know it. If we compare our system of knowledge with theirs then theirs is evidently the poorer one by far" (1969:286).

This is one of Wittgenstein's strongest statements against linguistic relativism. The people who believe we can go to the moon are, quite simply, wrong. They don't understand the limitations of our human form of life. Their concepts cannot create a reality in which what they believe can *become* reality. The fact that Wittgenstein got the limitations of our form of life wrong doesn't change his point here. What he doesn't take into account is that science and technology can radically change what appear to be firm limits on human possibility—like going to the moon. But even this consideration doesn't alter the fact that human life has limits; there are some things that we simply do or don't do. These limits are broad and subject to technological change, but they are not arbitrary. Our understanding of the relationship between language and reality must take account of these limits.

Philosophy is the battle against the bewitchment of our intelligence by means of language. (1958:§109)

What *we* do is to bring words back from their metaphysical to their everyday use. (1958:§116)

What, ultimately, is Wittgenstein trying to say about language? That it is central to human life, quite clearly. That the connection between language and reality assumed in the picture theory was misguided is also clear. But is he saying that *everything* is language, that language alone constitutes our reality as human beings? The linguistic turn of the twentieth century owes much to Wittgenstein's philosophy. His work is closely associated with this movement; indeed, he is seen as one of its principal authors. It is significant that proponents of SSK and ethnomethodology relied heavily on Wittgenstein's work to establish the thesis that the concepts of scientists create the reality that they study and thus that it is not necessary to go beyond those concepts in our analysis of science.

One of the most influential interpretations of Wittgenstein along these lines is that of Peter Winch in *The Idea of a Social Science and Its Relation to Philosophy* (1958). Winch applies the linguistic constructionist interpretation of Wittgenstein to the social sciences and concludes that social science should be a branch of philosophy:

Our language and our social relations are just two different sides of the same coin. To give an account of the meaning of a word is to describe how it is used; and to describe how it is used is to describe the social intercourses into which it enters. (1958:123)

Thus:

> It is not a question of what empirical research may show to be the case, but of what philosophical analysis reveals about *what it makes sense to say.* (72)

Winch's linguistic constructionism turns the social scientist into a linguistic analyst. For Winch there is no social reality out there that the social scientist studies, but rather, "Our idea of what belongs to the realm of reality is given for us in the language that we use" (15). It follows that

> Reality is not what gives language sense. What is real and what is unreal shows itself *in* the sense that language has. (1972:12)

It is important to stress the influence of this interpretation of Wittgenstein's work. His association with linguistic constructionism, particularly as it relates to the natural and the social sciences, has been enormous. But it is also important to note that in recent years interpreters of Wittgenstein are moving away from this interpretation. An example of this movement is the "practice theorists" discussed in chapter 1. In analyses that range from studies of scientific practice to anthropological studies, practice theorists focus on a broader perspective. Practice is something we *do*; it includes language, but it also includes the other aspects of human life: bodies, nature, biology. Practice theorists employ Wittgenstein's concept of "form of life" to explore the intermeshing of society and biology in ways of speaking and acting (Schatzki 1996).

It is this interpretation of Wittgenstein that I want to advance here. My thesis is that Wittgenstein is articulating what amounts to a version of the new settlement that Latour is advocating. That Wittgenstein is primarily interested in language is undeniable. But to read Wittgenstein as a linguistic constructionist is to seriously distort his work. His references to form of life, general facts of nature, and natural history indicate that he did not want to remove human beings from the material world in which we live. Instead, like Pickering, he wants to describe human life as a mangle constituted by the intra-action of the material and the discursive. The strongest evidence for this interpretation is his emphasis on language as a practice. For Wittgenstein language is not an abstract entity divorced from the rest of human life, particularly from the material world. Rather, it is embedded in human life, an integral part of what we do as real, material human beings.

The interpretation I am defending here raises two significant questions. First, why has Wittgenstein been so closely identified with the linguistic turn in philosophy? Why have a whole generation of theorists such as Winch and the SSK analysts interpreted Wittgenstein as a linguistic constructionist? The most obvious answer to this question is simply that Wittgenstein is almost exclusively concerned with language. He is a *linguistic* philosopher; he talks about little else. Thus using his work to ground the linguistic approach seemed, to many of his interpreters, quite obvious. Furthermore, it is easy to pull quotes out of context in Wittgenstein's work that can be used to support the linguistic constructionist position. Another answer to this question can be found by appealing to the power of the paradigm shift that characterizes contemporary thought. In the twentieth century philosophers turned almost exclusively to language. Discussion of "reality" or the material world was almost entirely off-limits because of their close association with modernity. Thus it should not be surprising that Wittgenstein's work was subsumed under this powerful sea change in philosophy. It seemed to fit very precisely within that paradigm.

The second question is why Wittgenstein's position on the relationship between language and reality is so vague. Why are his references to what we might want to call "reality" so sparse and enigmatic? Why does the language/reality interface in his work raise so many questions? If, as I am claiming, he is presenting an approach to this relationship that deconstructs this dichotomy, why is it not more clearly articulated? One answer to this question is simply that it was not his intention to do so. Wittgenstein wanted to show the errors of the picture theory, not to embrace or refute linguistic constructionism. Nor did he want to describe in detail the relationship between language and reality. These are our questions, functions of the horizon out of which we approach philosophical issues. But these are not Wittgenstein's issues. It should not be surprising, then, that we look for arguments that address this issue in his work. It should also not be surprising that these arguments are not to our satisfaction.

Another answer to this question is that it is very difficult to articulate the position I am calling the new settlement. If, as I am arguing that Wittgenstein does, we reject objectivism or realism as it was articulated in the early twentieth century, accept the role of language in the construction of reality, yet at the same time reject a strictly linguistic constructionist position, then defining that position is exceedingly difficult. How can we talk about the relationship between language and reality without falling into the twin errors of objectivism and linguistic relativism? What *is* reality if we reject both poles of this dichotomy?

Wittgenstein's vagueness on the definition of concepts such as form of life, natural history, and general facts of nature reflects this difficulty. Articulating the new settlement, as contemporary theorists are realizing, is a complicated undertaking. It requires balancing the role of language against that of the material world. Wittgenstein did not get very far in articulating this relationship. But asking Wittgenstein to address this issue is, in a sense, unfair. Wittgenstein was concerned primarily with the task of correcting the errors of the philosophy of his day. What I am calling the new settlement is a twenty-first-century problem, not one of the mid-twentieth century. What I am arguing, however, is that Wittgenstein's philosophy, far from laying the foundation for linguistic constructionism, points instead to a new understanding of the relationship between language and reality that privileges neither side of the dichotomy. It is this new understanding that is the task of contemporary theory. Those who are approaching this task can find a significant ally in Wittgenstein's work. And as one of the purported founders of linguistic constructionism, this ally is a crucial one indeed.

3

THE THIRD SETTLEMENT

Foucault — We Have Never Been Postmodern

If there is any group of thinkers who have been associated with linguistic constructionism, it is the philosophers commonly grouped under the label "postmodern" or "poststructuralist." In the contemporary intellectual world, postmodernism and poststructuralism are identified with the foundation of linguistic constructionism: the thesis that there is nothing but discourse. It is assumed that for these thinkers discourses create reality and even the subjects that inhabit that reality. Discourses, furthermore, are multiple and share no common universal standards. The result of these positions is at best relativism and at worst nihilism. Postmoderns and poststructuralists, it is assumed, have no possible bases for judgments, moral or epistemological, and reject the existence or even the possibility of "reality."

Like most generalizations, these are problematic on many levels. First there is the issue of who is a "postmodern" or "poststructuralist" and what, if any, differences separate the two positions. Few of the thinkers categorized by these labels are willing to accept the designation. Each defines his/her position as unique, defying any label. Then there is the problem of consistency. Is there a set of common themes that characterizes all the theorists placed under these labels? If so, what are they? Again, many of the theorists grouped under these categories would deny that such common themes exist. Probably the most we can assert is that there are "family resemblances," in Wittgenstein's sense, among the positions espoused by these thinkers.

It is not my intent here to answer these questions. Indeed, I do not think that it is worthwhile to spend theoretical energy attempting to do so. Instead, what I intend to do is to argue that one "postmodern" thinker, Michel Foucault, does not fit the commonly accepted profile of the "postmodern." It is worth noting at the outset that Foucault himself rejected the label, but this claim is not the basis of my argument. What I will argue is that Foucault, far from emphasizing discourse to the exclusion of the material or "reality," is, on the contrary, always acutely aware of the interaction between discourse and reality. I will argue that there is a reading of Foucault that puts him very close to the position of Latour and Pickering that I described in chapter 1. In short, my argument is that the quintessential postmodern, Michel Foucault, is not postmodern at all in the commonly accepted meaning of that term. Thus, borrowing shamelessly from Latour's title, I conclude that, at least in the case of Foucault, "we have never been postmodern."

A number of other commentators, principally utilizing the work of Giles Deleuze, have also argued that there is a reading of postmodernism that does not exclude the material. In focusing on the work of Foucault, I am not denying the validity of these arguments. The work of Deleuze, and particularly the work he co-authored with Guattari, departs from an exclusive focus on the linguistic in significant ways. The key concept in Deleuze and Guattari's impressive *A Thousand Plateaus* (1987) is that of the assemblage, a concept that challenges the basis of linguistic constructionism. Deleuze and Guattari define the assemblage as a multiplicity of flows that rejects the tripartite division between a field of reality (the world), a field of representation (the book), and a field of subjectivity (the author). Rather, an assemblage establishes conventions between certain multiplicities drawn from each of these orders (22–23). A collective assemblage joins enunciation, acts, statements, and incorporeal transformations attributed to bodies (88).

The concept of assemblage is closely linked to another key Deleuzian concept: experience. Assemblages, for Deleuze, are collective extensions of experience (Colebrook 2002:81). But Deleuze's concept of experience is far from the modernist concept of the given that is apprehended from a point of objectivity. Rather, experience for Deleuze is "transcendental": "Empiricism truly becomes transcendental . . . only when we apprehend directly in the sensible that which can only be sensed, the very being of the sensible: difference, potential difference, and difference in intensity as the reason behind qualitative diversity" (1994:56–57). Experience is transcendental for Deleuze not because it represents an objectively given reality but because it has no ground outside itself (Colebrook 2002:69).

Deleuze also rejects another founding concept of modernity: the constitutive subject. Subjectification, he declares, is an assemblage, not a condition internal to language (Deleuze and Guattari 1987:130). Subjects, furthermore, do not ground experiences. We cannot separate the subject from language, from the real, or from anything else. It is all just flows, and flows flow together. This does not mean that Deleuze is not aware of difference and diversity. Each multiplicity, he asserts, is already composed of heterogeneous elements in symbiosis, and each multiplicity is continuously transforming itself into a string of other multiplicities (Deleuze and Guattari 1987:249). But ultimately, for Deleuze, everything comes together in univocity, one univocal plane of being/becoming (Colebrook 2002:125).

That Deleuze is rejecting all the principal tenets of modernity is clear. Like Latour, he is seeking a new settlement that can address the problems caused by the modernist settlement. It is also clear that Deleuze is offering an alternative that does not privilege the linguistic at the expense of the material. On the contrary, for Deleuze everything comes together in his assemblages. What is not clear, however, is what Deleuze is actually arguing *for*. Those who find inspiration in his thought argue that the advantage of his position is that it opens everything up. For Deleuze, creating concepts means creating new ways of thinking. The task of philosophy, thus, is to create and maximize becoming against the recognition of becoming in any of its actualized forms (Colebrook 2002:26, 102). What interests Deleuze and Guattari, one commentator claims, is the circumstances created by the concepts they define. What they create, he declares, is "outside thought" (Massumi 1987:xiii).

The problem here is that Deleuze leaves us hanging in an ill-defined limbo. If everything is opened up and we are outside thought, where, exactly, are we? This problem becomes especially acute in the work of several admirers of Deleuze who have attempted to sketch out the political and ethical implications of his work. Claire Colebrook argues that Deleuze's contribution is that he questions the state. The advantage of Deleuze's thought, she argues, is that it allows us to think politics beyond the state (2002:148). But she cannot be any more specific than this vague statement. Michael Hardt, in an extended examination of a possible Deleuzian politics, argues that Deleuze's work provides the basis for radical democracy with a dynamic conception of democracy as open, horizontal, and collective. But even Hardt concludes that ultimately this vision is vague and roughly formulated. His assessment in the end is that Deleuze gives us only a hint of the democratic politics suggested by his work (1993:119–22).

William Connolly also looks to Deleuze for help in defining a politics that moves beyond both modernity and postmodernism. In *Neuropolitics* Connolly seeks to define "the politics through which cultural life mixes into the composition of body/brain processes" (2002:xiii). Like Deleuze, Latour, and Pickering, Connolly seeks to destabilize the nature/culture dualism in favor of a more interactive conception. In words reminiscent of Deleuze, Connolly argues:

> A multilayered conception of culture and thinking is needed today, one that comes to terms with how biology is mixed differentially into every layer of human culture, even as it addresses the highest modes of intellectuality, artistry, creativity, freedom and reflexivity of which the human animal is capable. (2002:62)

Connolly labels his position "immanent naturalism," a position that moves the transcendental to the immanent, resulting in "existential combination" (105). Two regulative ideas form the basis of Connolly's neuropolitics: "attachment to the earth and care for a protean diversity of being that is never actualized completely in any particular cultural setting" (197).

Hardt argues that Deleuze's politics are too vague, that they fail to provide even an outline of a concrete politics. I have the same problem with Connolly's Deleuzian-inspired politics. It is hard, if not impossible, to imagine what this politics would look like in the real world. How would Connolly's multilayered theory of nature/culture be translated politically? How would it change, if at all, the political practice we now have? How is care for the "protean diversity of being" actualized in political practices? Connolly, like Deleuze, is inspirational and compelling. We would all like to live in the world they describe. The problem is that it is hard to figure out what that world is or how we might get there. We need more than vague references to protean diversity to imagine the actual political change that Connolly and Deleuze desire.

Foucault provides a much better understanding of how a politics beyond both modernity and linguistic constructionism would be structured. Like Latour, Pickering, Deleuze, and Connolly, Foucault wants to describe a world in which nature and culture interact in complex ways. He wants to privilege neither the linguistic nor the material, but rather to integrate them in an interactive continuum. But unlike any of these thinkers, he offers a clear political vision that goes beyond vague generalities. His descriptions of prisons, hospitals, asylums, practices of sexuality, and many other elements of contemporary life give us a concrete sense of what our politics should be. He gives us, in short, something to do. In one of his more trenchant interviews, Foucault states: "My point is not that everything is bad, but that everything is dangerous, which is not exactly the same thing. If everything is dangerous then we will always have something to do. So my position leads not to apathy, but to a hyper- and pessimistic— activism" (1984:343).

Reinterpreting Foucault

The first element in my argument for a reinterpretation of Foucault rests on an analysis of his method. Foucault's method has been extensively discussed in the literature on his work. Much of this revolves around the distinction between genealogy and archaeology, the significance of the distinction, and an analysis of which of Foucault's works falls into which category. I will not pursue this discussion here. Rather, I will look at Foucault's method as a key to understanding the interaction of the discursive and the material in his work. What stands out in even a cursory analysis of both archaeology and genealogy is the intimate relationship between discourse and practice in both methods. Although the methods exhibit certain differences, they are more similar than different in their approach to this crucial relationship. Far from privileging either the linguistic or the material, Foucault's archaeology and genealogy integrate these elements in a distinctive method. As C. G. Prado puts it, "It is the actual consequences of actions that are the building blocks of archaeology's episteme and of genealogy's disciplinary techniques" (2000:29). Prado argues that what Foucault the archaeologist does is to reorder events not perceived before.

In the final chapter I will argue that the concept of disclosure is a useful way of characterizing the interaction of the discursive and the material in the production of knowledge. The definition of disclosure that I employ there is that of bringing to light, showing itself. Thus different aspects of reality can be disclosed from different perspectives. A careful analysis of Foucault's genealogical and archaeological methods yields an understanding very similar to disclosure. Foucault describes his goal as revealing a meaning in the already existent reality that had not been previously understood. In works such as *The Order of Things* (1970), he shows how changing concepts allow us to disclose the material world in new ways. Genealogy and archaeology are methods of that disclosure. One of the more striking descriptions of his method as a whole is his statement that what he is doing is a "history of the present." This history is a disclosure in the sense that it reveals a deeper understanding of the reality that is already there in contemporary life.

Foucault defines three domains covered by his genealogical method: the historical ontology of ourselves in reaction to truth through which we constitute ourselves as subjects of knowledge; the historical ontology of ourselves in relation to a field of power through which we constitute ourselves as subjects working on others; the historical ontology in relation to ethics through which we constitute ourselves as moral agents (1984:351). What stands out in this passage is the interrelationship of knowledge, ontology, and subjects in each of these domains. What Foucault is trying to accomplish in his genealogy is to describe precisely how these elements combine. Most importantly, his method entails that no single element in the combination has priority. For Foucault it is not the case that ontology trumps knowledge or vice versa, but rather they interact in complex ways to constitute subjects. In another context he argues that his method is the study of the play and development of a set of diverse realities articulated onto each other: a program, the connection that explains it, the law that gives it coercive power. These are all realities, he concludes, albeit in a different mode as the institutions that conform to them (1991a:81).

Perhaps the most notable analysis of Foucault's method is that of Hubert Dreyfus and Paul Rabinow in *Beyond Structuralism and Hermeneutics* (1982). This analysis is useful not only as a valuable interpretation of Foucault's work but also as an indication of the critical reception of his method. On one hand, Dreyfus and Rabinow argue that Foucault is always interested in discursive *practices*, how discourses are used, what role they play in society (1982:xxv). Although they argue that Foucault deviated from this principle in *The Order of Things* and *The Archaeology of Knowledge* by giving priority to discourse over practice, their overall emphasis is on the unity of discourse and practice in his work.[1] Dreyfus and Rabinow's conclusion is that Foucault gives an account of the unique way discourse is dependent upon, yet feeds back and influences, discursive practices (1982:67).[2]

On the other hand, however, Dreyfus and Rabinow do not entirely avoid the denial of the material that has become a staple of Foucault interpretation. In their conclusion to the discussion of Foucault's genealogy, they state: "In this discovery of groundlessness the inherent arbitrariness of interpretation is revealed" (1982:107). The definition of interpretation as arbitrary was a commonly held premise at the time Dreyfus and Rabinow were writing, so it should not be surprising that they attribute this position to Foucault. But their own analysis belies the validity of this interpretation. The point of genealogy, as they assert, is precisely that things are *not* arbitrary. The genealogist begins with the given, the way things are. It is then the genealogist's task to try to figure out not only what this given means but also how it became what it is. But in all of this the materiality of the subject matter is never in question.

> In fact, nothing is more material, physical, corporeal than the exercise of power. (Foucault 1980b:57)

The strongest element in my case for a reinterpretation of Foucault as a theorist of the interaction of the discursive and the non-discursive is his concern with power. It is not an exaggeration to say that Foucault is obsessed with power. He saw power everywhere. In fact, the theory of power that he develops posits precisely this: that power *is* everywhere. It is also not an exaggeration to say that Foucault transformed the study of power. Much has been and can be said about that transformation. My focus here will be his understanding of the materiality of power. As the above quote establishes, Foucault's understanding of power is very physical. He is concerned with how power affects us, particularly our bodies. But this is not all there is to the story. Foucault's understanding of power is also about the discourse of power. Indeed, his central thesis is that it was a significant change in the discourses of power that produced the unique form of power that characterizes the modern world. Foucault's analysis is about the complex interaction between the discursive and the non-discursive in the constitution of power. The goal of his analysis is to examine and explain this interaction.

The story that Foucault tells about power begins in the sixteenth century. From the end of the sixteenth century to the end of the eighteenth century, he declares, we see the development of a political rationality linked to a political technology:

> From the idea that the state has its own nature and its own finality to the idea of man as a living individual or man as a part of a population in relation to an environment, we can see the increasing intervention of the state in the life of individuals, the increasing importance of life problems for political power, and the development of possible fields for social and human sciences insofar as they take into account those problems of individual behavior inside the population and the relations between a living population and its environment. (1988b:160–61)

This passage lays out the broad parameters of Foucault's analysis. But the beauty of his analysis lies in the details and the intricate interweaving of discourse and practice that unfolded in these centuries. One of the central components of that development was the evolution of the police, a "project to create a system of regulation of the general conduct of individuals whereby everything would be controlled to the point of self-sustenance, without the need for intervention" (1984:241). Foucault links the evolution of this project to the Christian practice of what he calls "pastoral technology" (1988a:63). The police, like the pastors before them, are concerned with all aspects of human life and attempt to oversee all of those aspects. In short, "The police's true object is man" (79).

Foucault's thesis is that this radical change in the discourse of power had very real consequences. The state, through the police, moved into areas previously invisible to power: the body, sexuality, the family, kinship, knowledge, and technology. The most striking characteristic of these new technologies of power in the seventeenth and eighteenth centuries, Foucault asserts, is its concrete and precise character. Power is exercised through social production and social science. The new power had to have a real and effective incorporation; it had to gain access to individuals in their everyday behavior (1980b:122–25). This new type of power, Foucault concludes, is one of the great inventions of bourgeois society. Power in modern society is exercised both through the public right of sovereignty and "polymorphous disciplinary mechanisms" (106).

The brilliance of Foucault's analysis of power, however, lies not in these general comments, but rather in his very concrete analyses of key instances in the evolution of this power. *Madness and Civilization* (1965), *The Birth of the Clinic* (1973), and especially *Discipline and Punish* (1979) can be read as handbooks of the new power, graphic examples of both the nature of that power and how it spread throughout society. The diversity of these three analyses also illustrates Foucault's key thesis with regard to power: its multiplicity. Power as he describes it emanates from many different sources. It extends beyond the state, permeating multiple sources within society. Foucault's goal is to trace the transformation of power, not on the level of political theory, but "rather at the level of mechanisms, techniques, and technologies of power" (2003:241). These books analyze some of the major sources of that power, but they are not exhaustive in themselves. Power is everywhere; these are simply some of the major manifestations of that power in contemporary society.

Despite their differences, however, the technologies of power Foucault describes in these three books exhibit similar characteristics. By the end of the eighteenth century, he declares in *Madness and Civilization*, networks had spread over Europe: asylums, hospitals, prisons. "In a hundred and fifty years confinement had become the allusive amalgam of heterogeneous elements" (1965:44). Madmen were confined in asylums, sick people in hospitals, criminals in prisons. But this change did not come about willy-nilly. Nor was it the result solely of a change in discourse. Rather it was the result of the interaction, as Foucault puts it in *The Birth of the Clinic*, of words and things:

> In order to determine the moment at which the mutation in discourse took place, we must look beyond its thematic content or its logical modalities to the region

where "things" and "words" have not yet been separated, and where—at the most fundamental level of language—seeing and saying are still one. (1973:xi)

The unity of seeing and saying, the realm of disclosure, informs all of Foucault's analyses in these books.

Foucault's most compelling analysis of power is found in his impressive *Discipline and Punish* (1979). Confinement was an important first step in the evolution of the new form of power. Surveillance, the task of the prison, was the next. Although the techniques of surveillance were perfected in the prison, and particularly in the apparatus of Bentham's famous Panopticon, Foucault argues that these technologies did not stop at the prison's door. Rather, in one of his most controversial claims, Foucault argues that surveillance became the hallmark of power in our society. It spread to schools, barracks, hospitals, and other institutions. And significantly, it also became internalized. As a result of the ubiquitous practice of surveillance, each individual exercises surveillance over him/herself. We internalize the gaze that is everywhere (1980b:155). The result is the "carceral" society for which Foucault is so well known.

Surveillance produces discipline, and discipline is of bodies. Although bodies had appeared in previous books, it is in *Discipline and Punish* that they take center stage. Here Foucault asserts unequivocally that modern power is power over bodies, entities that had been all but ignored in previous regimes of power. The transformation of penal justice, Foucault argues, is the effect of the transformation of the way in which the body is invested in power relations. The subject of Foucault's book is the emergence of the political technology of the body (1979:24). Throughout his discussion, bodies are both real and fabricated, a product of discourse and material reality: "The individual is no doubt the fictitious atom of an 'ideological' representation of society; but he is also a reality fabricated by this specific technology of power that I have called 'discipline'" (1979:194).

What emerged through the disciplinary practices that Foucault describes is something he calls "bio-power." By bio-power Foucault means the techniques for achieving the subjugation of bodies and the control of populations. Bio-power is "what brought life and its mechanisms into the realm of explicit calculation and made knowledge-power an agent of transformation of human life" (1980a:143). The practices that Foucault categorizes under bio-power are very material and very specific. They reach individuals in their daily lives, in the details of their existence. They constitute a new "micro-physics of power" (1979:139), a "biopolitics of the human race" (2003:243). This biopolitics "included all devices that were used to ensure the spatial distribution of individual bodies (their separation, their alignment, their serialization, their surveillance) and the organization around those individuals of a whole field of visibility" (2003:242). In one of his most compelling metaphors, Foucault compares this kind of power to the spreading of capillaries:

> But in thinking of the mechanisms of power I am thinking rather of its capillary form of existence, the point where power reaches into the very grain of individuals, touches their bodies and inserts itself into their actions and attitudes, discourses, learning processes and everyday lives. The 18th century invented, so to speak, a synaptic regime of power, a regime of its exercise *within* the social body, rather than *from above it.* (1980b:39)

By bringing in the body, Foucault fundamentally changes our understanding of power. There are several levels to this transformation. First, political theorists had not, before Foucault, been concerned with bodies. By bringing bodies into the equation, Foucault introduces a new and distinctly material element into political theory. Second, for Foucault, the body is emblematic of power in the modern era. It is not just an aspect of power; it is the point where power is manifested in modern life. Third, the body for Foucault is not just a passive entity. Rather, bodies are at the same time constituted by disciplinary practices and the articulation of disciplinary power. The body is "the inscribed surface of events" (1977:148), the point of intersection of the disciplinary practices of modern power. Discipline "makes" individuals, and those individuals become the vehicle of disciplinary power (1979:170). Individuals are the effect of power but also the element of its articulation (1980b:98).

Disciplinary power reaches bodies through what Foucault calls the "apparatus." It is in the apparatus that the discursive and the non-discursive come together in the practices of power. Like Latour and Pickering, Foucault identifies the apparatus as a key component of the interface between language and materiality. The apparatus, for Foucault, is strategic; it is a particular manipulation of forces: "The apparatus is thus always inscribed in a play of power, but it is also always linked to certain coordinates of knowledge which issue from it but, to an equal degree, condition it" (1980b:196). When questioned regarding the distinction between the discursive and the non-discursive in the apparatus, Foucault is dismissive: he declares that making this distinction is not important. Pointing to the architectural plan of a military school, he asks: How can you separate the discursive from the non-discursive? To emphasize his point he concludes: "But I don't think it is very important to be able to make that distinction, given that my problem is not a linguistic one" (1980b:198).

Foucault claims that he is not offering a theory of power but rather an "analytics of power," the definition of the specific domain formed by relations of power and a determination of the instruments that make possible its analysis (1980a:82). But ultimately this claim makes little sense. Foucault's understanding of power is not only a theory, but it is a theory that fundamentally transforms our understanding of power. As Foucault himself says, "We need to cut off the king's head: in political theory that has still to be done" (1980b:121). Foucault's intention, clearly, is to accomplish this goal. For Foucault power is "a multiplicity of force relations," a "grid of intelligibility of the social order." Power is everywhere because it comes from everywhere; it is exercised from innumerable points, in the interplay of "nonegalitarian and mobile relations" (1980a:92–94).

In sum, there is no king; his head has been severed. Power is not a possession but a multifarious series of relations. Power passes through "finer channels"; it is more ambiguous (1980b:72). Most importantly for my purposes is Foucault's claim that we are subject to the production of truth through power. It is in the practices of power that knowledge and power are linked: "The exercise of power perpetually creates knowledge and, conversely, knowledge constantly induces effects of power" (52). The practices of power unite the discursive and the nondiscursive into an indistinguishable whole. Power is always already material. But it is also constituted by knowledge: "Knowledge and power are integrated with one another and there is no point of dreaming of a time when knowledge will cease to depend on power" (52).

For Foucault, power is inscribed on bodies, and bodies are turned into subjects. The issue of subjects and subjectification is at the very center of Foucault's theory of power. But the relationship between subjects and power is far from simple for Foucault. I have already discussed one aspect of that relationship: subjects are both the point of power's inscription and the vehicle of its articulation. This alone sets Foucault's view of the subject apart from what has become the "standard" postmodern view that subjects are social dupes. For Foucault, subjects are both acted on and act. Power is manifest in subjects, and subjects manifest power.

But there is an even more fundamental complexity in the subject's relationship to power. In order to *be* a subject, to have an ontological existence at all, one must be recognized *as* a subject in the discourses of one's society. Without the intersection of the body and the available discourses of subjectivity, one cannot, quite literally, *be* at all. This circumscribes subjects and subjectification in a radical way. It means that for subjects ontology has a unique link to discourse; no other entities are so linked. Another way of putting this is that the interface of the material and discursive is distinctive for subjects. The discursive enables the material in a way that does not apply to other beings.[3]

Foucault tries to grapple with this difficulty in his discussion of power and the subject:

> How is it that subjects are gradually, progressively, really and materially consti-
> tuted, through a multiplicity of organisms, forces, energies, materials, desires,
> thoughts etc. We should try to grasp subjection in its material instance as a consti-
> tution of subjects. (1980b:97)

In another context he attempts to clarify this point. It is not just in the play of symbols that subjects are constituted, he asserts, but in "real practices" that are historically analyzable (1984:369). This understanding of the subject and subjectification is most powerfully evident in Foucault's discussion of sex and sexuality. Rejecting the notion that there is a natural given to sexuality, Foucault asserts instead that it is a historical construct. This historical construct is "a great surface network" in which bodies and pleasure are linked "in accordance with a few major strategies of knowledge and power" (1980a:105–6). There is no baseline here; one can only *be* sexual according to the discourses of sexuality that wield power. But the result is nevertheless all too material. It is the reality in which all of us must define ourselves as sexual beings. It is the law of sex to which we must conform.

It is this reality that concerns Foucault and occupies his attention in his whole corpus. His goal is to attempt to uncover and explain that reality. He characterizes his goal as a "critical ontology":

> The critical ontology of ourselves has to be considered not, certainly, as a theory,
> a doctrine, nor even as a permanent body of knowledge that is accumulating; it
> has to be conceived as an attitude, an ethos, a philosophical life in which the
> critique of what we are is at the same time the historical analysis of the limits that
> are imposed on us and an experiment with the possibility of going beyond them.
> (1984:50)

Foucault's reference to ontology here and in other contexts is further evidence of his iconoclastic stance. Ontology is closely associated with the absolutism of modernity and is, as a consequence, rarely mentioned by postmoderns. Foucault, however, is not at all hesitant to embrace this concept. But what Foucault means by ontology is distinct from the modernist concept. For Foucault, ontology is not a fixed, given reality. It is not the baseline of reality from which we operate. Rather, it is a historical construct, a fluctuating and heterogeneous multiplicity. But this does not detract from its reality or, indeed, from its materiality. "What we are" is the product of history, discourse, bodies, nature, and many other factors. Our job as analysts is to determine how these forces interact to construct our reality. But that it is what we are is never in question.[4]

In the foregoing I have avoided an explicit discussion of an issue that most commentators would identify as the center of all of Foucault's work: the relationship between knowledge and power. This is not because I challenge this assessment. Rather, I want to approach this topic in the context of the above discussion of power and materiality. The basic parameters of Foucault's theory of knowledge and power are, again, well known: knowledge and power are intimately connected; knowledge produces power; it creates subjects; it subjectivizes. The knowledge/power nexus, furthermore, is ubiquitous to societies. We can never escape it; there is no libratory space beyond knowledge/power.

But there is more to Foucault's understanding of knowledge and power than these commonly accepted theses reveal. Almost in passing, Foucault makes a statement about the relationship between knowledge and power that suggests a different interpretation. If power were identical to knowledge, he declares, I would not have anything to study. The fact that they are *not* identical is the challenge: my goal, he asserts, is to analyze the *relationship* between knowledge and power (1988a:43). And this relationship, it turns out, is a very complicated one. Discourse transmits and produces power. But discourse is never separate from power: "Discourses are tactile elements or blocks operating in the field of force relations" (1980a:101). It is not possible to separate the discursive and the nondiscursive in this field. They intertwine and intermingle but never become identical.

Foucault provides a revealing example of how this interface operates in *The Birth of the Clinic* (1973). What changed at the end of the eighteenth century, he argues, is not the conception of disease but the relation between disease and the gaze. There is no distinction between theory and experience: "One had to read the deep structure of visibility in which field and gaze are bound together by *codes of knowledge*" (1973:90). The clinical gaze, Foucault concludes, is a perceptual act sustained by a logic of operations: "The gaze of observation and the things it perceives communicate through the same Logos" (109). For clinical experience to become possible as a form of knowledge, a reorganization of the hospital field and a new definition of the patient was required. Discursive and nondiscursive had to operate in tandem (196).

Throughout his work Foucault characterizes this relationship in different ways. One is the use of spatial metaphors. Describing discourse through spatial metaphors, he argues, enables one to grasp the point at which discourses are transformed "in, through and on the basis of power" (1980b:70). Another strategy is to describe discourse as an *event*. Events are neither substance nor accident, yet an event is not immaterial. It takes effect on the level of the material. Events

> consist in relation to, coexistence with, dispersion of, the cross-checking accumulation and selection of material elements; it occurs as an effect of, and in, material

>dispersion. Let us say that the philosophy of event should advance in the direction, at first paradoxical, of an incorporeal materialism. (1972b:231)

Discursive events involve a play of interdependencies: intra-discursive, inter-discursive, and extra-discursive. My question, Foucault asserts, is not about codes of language but about *events* (1991a:58–59).[5]

What this comes to, then, is that for Foucault the discursive and the non-discursive merge into the event. There is no clear line between the two, and the attempt to draw such a line misrepresents the phenomenon. This interpretation of Foucault's corpus works well for most of his work. But two books stand out as exceptions. In *The Order of Things* (1970) and *The Archaeology of Knowledge* (1972), it appears that Foucault focuses exclusively on discourse, denying the material in "standard" postmodern fashion. As I noted above, Dreyfus and Rabinow explain these books by arguing that Foucault, in a sense, lost his way in writing them. He was seduced by discourse and, giving discourse priority, essentially ignored the material.

There is another way of reading these books, however. Their focus, clearly, is discourse. But in focusing on discourse, Foucault never loses sight of the connection between the discursive and the non-discursive. It is not inconsistent to maintain, as I think Foucault does in these works, both that the discursive and the non-discursive are inextricably intertwined and that it is possible to focus on one or the other in the course of a particular analysis. As an analyst I can choose to focus on a particular aspect of a phenomenon without denying the existence or even the importance of other aspects of that phenomenon. One could argue, for example, that in *Discipline and Punish, The Birth of the Clinic,* and *Madness and Civilization* Foucault focuses on the material rather than the discursive. But in these works, as in all his writings, the interface between the two is the ground of the analysis.

The title of the original French edition of *The Order of Things* translates as "words and things." This title captures much more clearly what Foucault is trying to do in the book. Foucault's analysis of the changing epistemes is a story of how words and things interact, not the story of how language constitutes reality. In the introduction he states that in every culture there is, between the use of the ordering codes and the reflection on order, the "pure experience of order and its modes of being" (1970:xxi). The fundamental codes provide us with the empirical order that allows us to be at home in the world. The aim of his analysis, Foucault asserts, is to define what made it possible for opinions about language to exist at all, to show how language intertwines with what is exterior and indispensable to it (119).

There is a lot of discussion of being and modes of being in *The Order of Things*. The apriori, Foucault claims, is what, in a given period, delineates in the totality of experience a field of knowledge and defines the mode of being of objects (1970:158). And "Before this language of language, it is the thing itself that appears, in its own characters, but within the reality that it has patterned from the very outset by the name" (130). He talks about things touching against the "banks of discourse," appearing in the hollow space of representation (130). Later, describing the emergence of philology, biology, and political economy, he asserts that they appeared in the spaces that were left blank, the gaps filled by the "murmur of the ontological continuum" (207).

A blurb on the back of the English paperback version of *The Order of Things* declares that the book "reveals the shocking arbitrariness of our received truths." What this blurb reveals is indeed a received truth, but it is one about Foucault, not his subject in this book. The publishers are expressing the accepted interpretation of *The Order of Things*: that knowledge is arbitrary, that discourses create the reality they describe. What I am suggesting here is that if we read the book in the context of Foucault's work as a whole, a very different interpretation is possible. Foucault's point is that the changing discourses he describes reveal different modes of being. They do not constitute that being, but rather, in the sense I am using the word, they disclose it. And importantly, he never questions that the material reality is there to *be* disclosed. Our concepts apprehend that reality in very different ways, but for Foucault there is always something there—the ontological continuum, being or its modes—to be disclosed.

A similar interpretation can be applied to *The Archaeology of Knowledge*. The goal of the book, Foucault declares, is to remain at the level of discourse. Discourses, he asserts, are practices; they exist in a field of non-discursive practices; statements have materiality (1972a:49, 68, 105). Again, the message is clear: the discursive and the non-discursive are linked. The aim of archaeology, even though it is primarily concerned with discourses, is the systematic description of the "discourse-object" (1972a:140). As Deleuze puts it in his discussion of *The Archaeology of Knowledge*, for Foucault the statement has primacy, but primacy does not mean reduction (1988:49). What we are left with, finally, is a version of disclosure. Objects exist under the positive conditions of a complex group of relations—economic, social, and so on. These relations are not present in the object but are what enable it to appear, "to be placed in a field of exteriority" (1972a:45).

In his last books, Foucault turns to an issue that he sees to be at the heart of his attempt to construct a history of the present: the self. Foucault wants to know how our particular conception of the self evolved. He examines the key elements in this development and how this conception came to have the specific characteristics that mark it today, characteristics that define our civilization. This explanation takes him far beyond the issues that had previously occupied his attention. He now turns to ancient civilization, their texts and practices, in order to answer his questions. It is a departure for him, but not in the sense that he departs from the basic presuppositions that guided his work from the outset. The discourses he examines, discourses that establish the parameters of selfhood in the West, were at the same time material practices, activities in which individuals engaged. The unity and inseparability of knowledge and power, the discursive and the non-discursive, still guides the analysis.

If anything, Foucault seems even more committed to this thesis than in his earlier work. Listen to him in *The Uses of Pleasure*:

> The relation to truth was a structural, instrumental, and ontological condition for establishing the individual as a moderate subject leading a life of moderation; it was not an epistemological condition enabling the subject to recognize himself in his singularity as a desiring subject and to purifying himself as the desire that was thus brought to light. (1985:89)

What Foucault accomplishes in these books, in a sense, is a widening of the scope of his analysis of the relationship between knowledge and power. In his previous work he was concerned with governmental or quasi-governmental institutions: asylums, hospitals, prisons. Now he is turning to more explicitly social relations. Sexual activity is regulated in a different way than the activities Foucault had previously studied. As he notes in *The Care of the Self*, the control of sexual activity was regulated not by a strengthening of public authority, but in philosophy. The care of the self that developed in the ancient world and has come to define the West was a *social practice* (1986:51). Once more, Foucault is illustrating his central thesis: power is everywhere; it does not stop with the political but extends into the interstices of our lives.[6]

⟜

The foregoing analysis leaves one important question unanswered: if my interpretation is correct and Foucault, far from forgetting the material, integrates it into every aspect of his analysis, how has his work come to represent precisely the opposite, the primacy of discourse, the discursive construction of reality? I addressed a similar question with regard to the interpretation of Wittgenstein that I am advancing. If anything, the question is even more pressing in Foucault's case. For a whole generation of thinkers, Foucault stands for linguistic constructionism and all it entails: relativism, nihilism, arbitrariness, and the abandon-ment of all standards—physical, epistemological, and moral. This judgment is so widespread that it demands some explanation.

There are several ways to answer this question. The first is similar to that which I offered in the case of Wittgenstein: a picture held us captive. But Fou-cault's relationship to the picture is different from that of Wittgenstein. Witt-genstein was writing before linguistic constructionism was firmly established. Foucault, in contrast, was writing at a time when the linguistic turn was all-pervasive. We *wanted* to read Foucault as a linguistic constructionist because we read everyone from this perspective. And in the case of Foucault it was not difficult to do so. Foucault's work, like that of Wittgenstein, is all about lan-guage, discourses, and how they structure the world around it. He is concerned with how discursive changes cause us to see a different world. He discusses these discourses and these changes at great length in his books. Reading this through the lens of linguistic constructionism, it is not difficult to come to the conclusion that Foucault shares these beliefs. It is also not difficult to ignore evidence to the contrary.

The second answer is more complicated. It is undeniable that Foucault is reacting against the essentialism of modernity, the effort to find universal truth and to define a given, objective world. But it does not necessarily follow from this that he embraces linguistic constructionism, relativism, and nihilism. In the foregoing analysis I have tried to demonstrate that the material world is centrally important for Foucault. He is intimately concerned with the realities of the social and political world. But he is also concerned with the way in which discourses shape those realities and how they change as knowledge changes.

What Foucault is attempting to do, then, is far from simple. He wants to question universal truth and to explore how language, discourse, and knowledge shape our world. But he also wants to talk about the material parameters of that world and how that materiality interacts with discourses. It is not insignificant that in his early life Foucault flirted with Marxism. There is an element of Marx's concern with the material that lingers in his work. It is also significant that Al-thusser, who studied under many of the same teachers as Foucault, comes up with a position which, although explicitly Marxist, is in some sense not far from Foucault's own.[7]

What I am arguing, then, is that Foucault has been misunderstood because of the difficulty and complexity of his position. Like Latour, Pickering, Barad, and the other thinkers I am discussing here, Foucault is trying to integrate the insights of the linguistic turn while retaining reference to the material. This is not an easy position. It requires an intellectual repositioning that is difficult to accomplish. Foucault has been classified as a linguistic constructionist because there are elements in his thought that lend themselves to this interpretation. This interpretation is easier than the one I am suggesting here. Trying to figure out what Foucault is saying about knowledge and materiality requires going into what Althusser calls a "new continent of thought" and Latour calls a new settlement. Not everyone who reads his work is willing to make that intellectual leap.

Finally, what I am arguing about both Wittgenstein and Foucault is that a reinterpretation of their work is significant for the articulation of the new settlement in two senses. First, both offer an understanding of the relationship between discourse and the material that is complex and challenging. The substance of their work provides important insights into this relationship that is at the center of the new settlement. Second, because both Wittgenstein and Foucault have been installed as founding fathers of the linguistic constructionism that has taken the academic world by storm, my reinterpretation constitutes a significant challenge to that position. If Wittgenstein and Foucault can be shown to support a very different position on the relationship between discourse and the material, then linguistic constructionism loses much of its cogency.

4

THE FOURTH SETTLEMENT

Feminism—From Epistemology to Ontology

> I, and others, started out wanting a strong tool for deconstructing the truth claims
> of hostile science by showing the radical historical specificity, and so contestability,
> of every layer of the onion of scientific and technological constructions, and we
> end up with a kind of epistemological electro-shock therapy, which far from
> ushering us into the high stakes tables of the game of contesting public truths,
> lays us out on the table with self-induced multiple personality disorder.
>
> —*Haraway 1991:186*

Feminists have always had a special relationship with science. A central aspect
of that relationship, as Haraway indicates in this passage, is science's hostility to
women in general and feminists in particular. What might be called the first
wave of feminist critiques of science focused on this hostility. The work of Haraway, Harding, Longino, Code, Keller, and many others transformed science
studies. These works criticized the exclusion of women from the institution
of science and the sexist bias of scientific investigations. They called into question scientific practice at its most basic level. Revealing the sexism of science
uncovered the heretofore hidden dimension of scientific research, thus challenging the claim to objectivity that grounds scientific knowledge. What Haraway here calls "epistemological electro-shock therapy" was very effective. Feminist critics of science, in conjunction with those philosophers of science who

problematized the objectivity of scientific knowledge, fundamentally redefined our view of science.

But as Haraway is also aware, this therapy has its down side. She notes: "The further I get with the description of the radical social constructionist program and a particular version of postmodernism coupled to the acid tools of critical discourse in the human sciences, the more nervous I get" (1991:185). In a sense, the feminist critique of science, a critique that definitively established the social construction of scientific knowledge, was a victim of its own success. If everything, including scientific knowledge, is a social construction, then, as Haraway puts it, we are subject to multiple-personality disorders. In short, we replace Truth with truths and thus lose any grounding in the real. No statement, scientific or otherwise, has any priority over any other statement: all are equally vulnerable to critique because all are social constructions. As Searle (1995) so aptly points out, if everything, including science, is a social construction, allegations of social construction become meaningless.

Haraway is not the only feminist who is dissatisfied with this outcome. There is an interesting parallel here between feminism and science: neither can afford to give up on the real material world. Scientists cannot give up because their job is to make true statements about that world. If there is no way to distinguish true from false statements about the world, or even worse, if "the real" is a relative concept, then the practice of science loses its purpose. Feminists have a different but equally compelling reason for holding on to the real: the necessity of making true statements about the reality of women's lives— their oppression, their inferior social status, the pain inflicted on their bodies. Without the ability to make true statements about women's lives, feminism, like science, makes little sense.

The question that Haraway and other feminists are grappling with, however, is how to find a new approach, a new settlement in Latour's sense, that could address this problem. By the beginning of the twenty-first century, feminism's investment in critiques of science that focus on its social construction is significant.[1] Even though some feminists are, like Latour, coming to the conclusion that this critique is leading feminism down the wrong path, what a new path might be is, as for science, not clear.[2] The dis-ease among even the established feminist critics of science, however, is palpable. Feminist critics of science who were pioneers in establishing the social construction of scientific knowledge are starting to reformulate their positions.

Sandra Harding's means of addressing these issues is to argue that standpoint theories should avoid the excessive constructionism and consequently the damaging relativism that have plagued less materialist grounded accounts. Her alternative is a "constructionist materialism" (2004:38). Ann Fausto-Sterling (2000) takes a different but related tack. Fausto-Sterling focuses on dichotomies—between sex and gender, nature and nurture, social and physical—and argues that we should adopt an anti-dualist approach. Promoting what she calls "Developmental Systems Theory" and "connectionism," Fausto-Sterling argues for scientific analysis that can answer the question how does the social become material? The strength of her perspective is revealed in her insightful analysis of what may seem an unlikely topic: bones. Employing what she calls a "live-course analysis," Fausto-Sterling argues that bones are particularly useful in manifesting the interaction of nature and culture in human life. Bones reveal how our bodies imbibe culture, how nature and culture merge in our bodies' materiality (2005).

Helen Longino (2002) also sees dichotomies as the principal problem. Social studies of science, she asserts, are presumed on an absolute dichotomy: either nature imposes its character directly on our cognitive processes or scientists' cognitive processes are mediated in various ways. Longino's thesis is that we need to overcome this dichotomy. Citing the work of Latour, she argues that it is not possible to create knowledge by fiat; the natural world must have input (2002:35). The key to Longino's account is her attempt to rescue or redefine reason. Noticing the social and cultural embeddedness of scientists and their reasoning, she asserts, does not banish reason from science (37). Rather, it leads to the conclusion that rationality and sociality are equally aspects of knowledge (143).

In 2004 *Hypatia* published a special issue on feminist approaches to science. In the introduction to the volume, Lynn Hankinson Nelson and Alison Wylie (2004:x) argue that in contemporary feminist science studies an unqualified social constructionism is just as inadequate as objectivism. Most contemporary feminist critics of science would probably agree with this assessment. What they would not agree on, however, are the parameters of an approach that avoids both of these extremes. What this approach entails, its importance for feminism and critical thought as a whole, is the subject of this chapter and this book. My thesis is that feminist theorists have developed a highly significant "settlement" of the issues posed by modernity and postmodernism. I am further arguing that this feminist settlement has the most potential for solving the questions posed by the crisis in knowledge currently under way. Because of the uniquely situated character of feminist critique, feminist theorists have developed an approach that offers the clearest definition of the new critical path that is emerging. Although the other settlements discussed here add important elements to the critical project, the feminist settlement is the most comprehensive. It addresses epistemological, ontological, political, scientific, and technical issues simultaneously. It is concerned, not just with science, knowledge, or power, but with all of these at once, and most importantly, with the interaction among them. More clearly than any of the other settlements it indicates the direction that further critique will take.

At this point in the discussion the new approach does not have an agreed-upon label. Many have been proposed: several feminist critics of science favor "the new materialism"; Nancy Tuana proposes "interactionism" and "viscous porosity"; Karen Barad favors "intra-action" and "agential realism." The lack of consensus on a label, however, is indicative of little more than the newness of the approach. What is important is that there is a building consensus among feminists and critical theorists that a new approach is needed and that feminism is and should be on the forefront of that effort.

Donna Haraway, not surprisingly, has provided a bridge from the "old" feminist critiques of science to a new perspective. Although Haraway's work almost defined the social constructionist approach to science for a generation of feminist theorists, she was never entirely happy with social constructionism. From the outset she raised questions about the viability of an unqualified embrace of social constructionism. For Haraway it was always important to retain some connection to the real, some connection to scientific truth. Even in her early work she declared that we must develop an account that simultaneously accounts for the radical historical contingency of all knowledge and provides a "no-nonsense" commitment to faithful accounts of the real world (1991:187). She provides a striking metaphor for this task: finding a useable doctrine of objectivity, she claims, is like climbing a greased pole (188). Her solution, situated knowledge, defined feminist science studies for a generation of feminists.

Nearly a decade later, in *Modest Witness* (1997), Haraway is still committed to situated knowledges, but she wants to revise her perspective in important ways. What we need now, she declares, is a "materialized refiguring," a position that is not relativism but "a principled refusal of the stacked deck that forces a choice between loaded dualities such as realism and relativism" (1997:68). Overcoming these dualisms, for Haraway, entails simultaneously claiming that "the world takes shape in specific ways and cannot take shape just any way" (143) and that reality is collectively, materially, and semiotically constructed (301).

Haraway's work has been iconic in the evolution of feminist critiques of science. Her groundbreaking work in the 1980s and 90s laid the basis for the first generation of feminist critiques. Her current work, similarly, provides the impetus for the new generation of critiques that is emerging. The key to the new direction these critiques are taking is a movement anticipated by Haraway: the movement from epistemology to ontology. Epistemology was the focus of social constructionism. Critiques emphasized the production of knowledge from an exclusively discursive perspective. The new generation of feminist theorists is arguing that the obsession with epistemology that characterized social constructionism is a dead end. Epistemology is of necessity about representation, and representation is necessarily about dichotomies. Representation gives us two choices: knowledge is either objective or subjective. As long as we remain within the purview of epistemology, this dichotomy is inescapable. Haraway is right: we are trying to climb a greased pole. What she does not emphasize sufficiently is that this attempt is doomed to failure. It is now becoming clear that the only solution is to abandon the pole altogether.[3]

This thesis is forcefully stated in Sharyn Clough's important work *Beyond Epistemology* (2003). Clough's premise is that philosophy/epistemology is not the most effective focus for feminists engaged in science criticism. She begins with the assertion that "our investment in an epistemological critique is beginning to yield diminishing returns" (2003:2). Feminist epistemology, she claims, is caught up in the skepticism that informs all epistemological inquiry. It falls prey to what she calls the "representationalist model" of the relationship between knowers and the world. This model will always be unsatisfactory because we do not have direct access to the empirical world that causes our representations (13).

Clough's solution, like that of Rouse, is to abandon representationalism altogether. As a means of accomplishing this goal, she advocates adopting the pragmatism of Richard Rorty and Donald Davidson.[4] Both correspondence and coherence theories, the current options in epistemology, are representationalist. The only alternative, she claims, lies in seeing beliefs, not as faulty representations of the external world, but as a triangulation between language users and shared features of their world. An important consequence of this view is that we must have *some* true beliefs (2003:14). Building on this insight, Clough defines her goal as convincing feminists engaged in science studies to shift back to empirically focused work. This shift would be based on the assurance that our concepts of objectivity and truth are not in need of philosophical reconfiguration.

Clough grounds her position in Davidson's theory of a web of beliefs.[5] She adopts Davidson's thesis that we operate in a shared background of true beliefs and it is from this background that we can identify false beliefs. Davidson posits an interaction between concepts and their application. His theory is that we do not form concepts and then discover their application. Rather, the application determines the content of the concept. It also follows that all of our concepts cannot be up for grabs at once, only some can be. You have to be right about a large background of beliefs before you can critically examine the validity of particular ones (2003:103–8).

Clough's application of Davidson's theory to feminism is clear and forceful. First, "There is only one world, an objective view of which can be made meaningful only by the language users who are a part of it" (2003:117). Second, "Our scientific theories and our beliefs about oppression and justice are not merely relative to our feminist conceptual scheme, they are justified by the evidence and they are true" (127). Clough began her argument by claiming that Rorty and Davidson sidestep the problems of representationalism. It is clear that her position succeeds in sidestepping the problems encountered by the first generation of feminist critics of science. On Clough's view we need not continually apologize for the situatedness of feminist knowledge. For Clough and Davidson, all knowing is interaction between language and the world, an interaction that is grounded in true belief. The metaphor of the greased pole is replaced by the metaphor of the background.[6]

The New Feminist Settlement

Clough's work has the virtue of laying out very clearly the theoretical direction of feminist science criticism that she advocates. Her assault on epistemology is unambiguous and forceful, and at the end of her book Clough strongly exhorts feminists to move in the new theoretical direction she has outlined. But Clough does not move beyond the theoretical dimension. She does not indicate how this new approach would change feminist analyses in practice. However, it is precisely in the application of this new approach that its strength lies. There are two feminist theorists working today who bring theory and practice together in their discussions and thus reveal the full dimensions of the new approach. Nancy Tuana and Karen Barad offer clear and compelling theoretical arguments, but they also show how these arguments play out in the real world of the political, economic, material, and scientific. Their work provides decisive substantiation of the claim I am making here: that the feminist settlement is the most powerful articulation of the new approach.

The work of Nancy Tuana has been at the forefront of defining a new approach for feminist theory and practice for several decades. Like Clough, Tuana is very clear about the necessity of transcending the dualisms that structure philosophical discussions. Since her pathbreaking article in *Hypatia*, "Re-fusing Nature/Nurture" (1983), Tuana has made these dualisms the focus of her attention. This early article assessed the nature/culture dualism. In subsequent work one of her favorite targets has been the sterility of the realism/anti-realism debate. Feminist work in epistemology and science studies, Tuana argues, has begun to identify the need for a close and nuanced examination of the complexities of materiality, specifically the cognitive impact of embodiment and the relationship between human materiality and the more-than-human world

(2001:221). The alternative that Tuana suggests is "interactionism," a position that describes the emergent interplay of materiality.

Tuana takes on the central issue of epistemology and ontology directly. Like Clough, she is dissatisfied with the correspondence/coherence options, arguing that we need a theory that posits the "coherence of interpretation, practice, phenomena, and materials" (2001:228). The means of accomplishing this, Tuana argues, is to change our focus from epistemology to ontology. Against the social constructionist account she argues for a "new metaphysic" that grounds human ways of knowing in patterns of bodily being:

> Neither the materiality of the more-than-human world, nor human materiality is an unchanging given. What exists is emergent, issuing from complex interactions between embodiment and the world. (238)

Tuana's approach constitutes a bold philosophical move. She not only clearly defines the problem facing feminism and critical thought more generally, but she lays out a carefully defined alternative. Her "new metaphysic" addresses the key issues facing both philosophy and feminist theory. At the center of this metaphysics is her emphasis on embodiment. For Tuana, we always know as embodied human beings. This allows her to overcome the dualisms that plagued modernity: nature and culture, human and nonhuman, the discursive and the material. For Tuana, everything is always in flux; the human, more-than-human, material, and discursive are interacting in a complex mix. The result is a transformation of our understanding of knowledge and the world that is revolutionary.

But this is not all there is to Tuana's work. What makes her approach so exceptional is her application of this theory to very real world events. The best example to date of Tuana's brilliant interweaving of theory and practice is her recent analysis of hurricane Katrina. In "Viscous Porosity: Witnessing Katrina" (2008), Tuana brings her theory to bear on the events surrounding the hurricane's destruction in New Orleans. Tuana's analysis is grounded in the philosophical position she has outlined in her previous work, a position she now labels "viscous porosity." But what makes her analysis transformative is how she describes the array of forces that constitute the event we call Katrina. These forces include the economic, the political, the ecological, the biological, the historical, and the racial. Tuana's analysis encompasses, among many other elements, the political environment that structured the disaster, the chemical composition of the flood waters, even the effect of the shell middens that the Native Americans gathered before the influx of white settlers. It is a striking example of Pickering's mangle played out on the scene of an event with which we are all familiar. Tuana's work graphically reveals the complexity and resourcefulness of the "new metaphysic." Her analysis of Katrina provides a kind of template for how we can integrate the disparate elements that constitute our new understanding of knowledge.

Karen Barad, like Tuana, offers an array of concepts to describe her approach. These include "intra-action," "agential realism," "performativity," and "onto-epistem-ology." Beginning in the mid-1990s, Barad published a series of articles that outlined the parameters of her approach. Then, in 2007, she published *Meeting the Universe Halfway: Quantum Physics and the Entanglement of Matter and Meaning*. This book provides the definitive statement of her theory. It also provides the definitive statement of what I am calling the feminist settlement. Her approach offers feminists and science critics a wholly new way to address questions of truth and knowledge. Her theory breaks new ground not only for feminists but for all theorists concerned with the future direction of knowledge.

The impetus for Barad's theory is her conviction that language has become the exclusive focus of contemporary thought to the exclusion of all other elements: "Language has been granted too much power. The linguistic turn, the semiotic turn, the interpretive turn, the cultural turn: it seems that at every turn lately every 'thing'—even materiality—is turned into a matter of language or some other form of cultural representation" (2007:132). In this and other passages, Barad has in a sense thrown down the gauntlet against the current orthodoxy, particularly in feminist theory. The "turns" she cites here—linguistic, semiotic, interpretive—have dominated feminist and critical thought for the last several decades. Taking on this orthodoxy, as Barad is all too aware, will not be easy. It will also not be popular. A whole generation of feminist scholars has been taught to put "matter" in scare quotes. Removing those scare quotes, making matter matter, as Barad puts it, will be no mean feat.

This daunting task, however, is precisely the goal of *Meeting the Universe Halfway*. Barad begins the book by declaring: "Matter and meaning are not separate elements" (2007:3). The subject of her book, thus, is "entanglements": to be entangled is not simply to be intertwined with another, but "to lack an independent, self-contained existence . . . individuals emerge through and as a part of their entangled intra-relating" (ix). The thesis that Barad develops throughout her book is that quantum physics can show us how entanglement works; it can lead us out of the morass that takes absolutism and relativism as the only two possibilities (18).

What Barad offers in the course of her impressive book is what she claims is a deeper understanding of the ontological dimension of scientific practice. This entails, most centrally, a redefinition of realism. Realism, she asserts, "can offer a possible ballast against the persistent positivist scientific and postmodernist cultures that too easily confuse theory with play" (2007:43). The notion of constructing a "ballast" gets to the heart of Barad's project: resisting the trend of contemporary theorizing not to take matter seriously. Her reference to "play" is also significant. It is a thinly veiled reference to the work of Derrida, whose influence in feminist thought has been pervasive and, Barad would argue, pernicious. What Barad wants to do is to provide a counter to these tendencies, to resist the move to play that she sees as taking feminism away from its serious subject matter: matter. Barad realizes the difficulty of the task of challenging an established orthodoxy. But she is convinced that her goal, giving an account of materiality as an active and productive factor in its own right, is essential to the future of feminism.

In order to formulate her approach, Barad turns to the work of Niels Bohr. Bohr's theoretical position is centered around what he calls "agential reality." Like Pickering, Bohr attributes agency to matter, but specifically, in Bohr's case, matter that has been given agency by a theory. On Bohr's view, scientific theories describe agential reality; that is, different theories make different aspects of matter agential. Bohr's example is light defined as particles vs. waves: it is impossible to describe particles and waves simultaneously because mutually exclusive experimental arrangements are required (Barad 2007:106). For Barad, Bohr's agential realism has the advantage of bringing matter back in, and specifically matter as agential, without denying the role of theory in the constitution of what will become "reality" (97–131).

Bohr's work has another advantage for Barad as well: his emphasis on the apparatus. For Bohr, measurement and description entail one another: "Concepts are defined by the circumstances required for their measurement" (2007:109). It follows that "there is no unambiguous way to differentiate between the object and the agencies of observation. No inherent/Cartesian subject-object distinction exists" (114). In the course of her work Barad offers a reformulation of Bohr's theory of apparatuses that focuses on the specific material-discursive practices of the apparatus and their material reconfiguration of the world (146). What she will call the "intra-action" among theory, apparatus, and the material is the center of her approach.

In one of her early articles Barad identifies what she sees to be the principal advantages of agential realism. First, it grounds and situates knowledge claims in local experience. Thus objectivity is literally embodied. Second, agential realism privileges neither the material nor the cultural; rather, production is material/cultural. Third, agential realism entails the interrogation of boundaries and cultural reflexivity. Drawing different boundaries has different ontological implications. Fourth, agential realism underlines the necessity of an ethic of knowing; our constructed knowledge has real, material consequences (1996:179–83).

For Barad, agential realism is a form of social construction, but it is not relativist, nor does it reject objectivity. She concludes: "Realism is not about representations of an independent reality, but about the real consequences, interventions, creative possibilities, and responsibilities of intra-acting within the world" (188).

Agential realism as Barad defines it provides a powerful alternative to the dominant orthodoxy of linguistic constructionism. Barad's assertion is that postmodernism and poststructuralism claim to deconstruct dichotomies such as nature/culture and material/discursive; but in fact they fail to do so, instead privileging the culture/discourse side of the dichotomies. From this perspective Barad's theory does what postmodernism and poststructuralism only claim to do: it overcomes these dichotomies and provides a framework that "takes as its central concern the nature of materiality, the relationship between the material and the discursive, the nature of 'nature' and 'culture,' the relationship between them, the nature of agency, and the effects of boundary, including the nature of exclusions that accompany boundary projects" (1998:89). In her book, Barad makes it clear that her commitment to agential realism entails an attack on representationalism, an attack that has characterized many of the "settlements" I am examining. Agential realism, she claims, shifts the focus from the nature of representation to the nature of discursive practices. Instead, it examines how discursive practices are related to material phenomena (2007:45).

The movement away from representationalism is at the same time a movement toward ontology. Barad's approach to ontology is one of the significant strengths of her theory. In contrast to postmodernism and poststructuralism, ontology is the focal point of agential realism. Postmoderns and poststructuralists rejected ontology because of its association with modernity. But Barad's "ontology" is not the ontology of modernity. For Barad, agential realism is not a fixed ontology that is independent of human practices but is continually reconstituted through our material-discursive intra-actions (2007:136–41). To emphasize this difference, Barad suggests replacing ontology with a new term: "onto-epistemology," the study of the practices of knowing (44).

Postmoderns reject ontology not only because of its association with modernism but also because of their conviction, if they can be said to have convictions, that "there is no there there," it is all fiction, play. Barad's counter is that there *is* a there there, but it is fluid rather than fixed. But there is another aspect to Barad's approach to ontology that is of paramount importance, especially for my purposes: her assertion that theories have material consequences. Theories, discourse, give matter agency, and that agency matters in a very real sense. The agency of matter structures the reality of our world. It sets the boundaries of that reality, establishing what is included and excluded from the real. These bound-

aries have very real political, economic, social, and material consequences. Perhaps the greatest strength of Barad's theory is that she can account for these
consequences in the complexity of her approach.

Barad characterizes the operation of agential realism as "intra-action."
This term is her attempt to describe the inseparability of objects and agents of
observation in agential realism. She cites Foucault's work on disciplinary power
as an example of intra-action. For Foucault disciplinary power is exercised
through various apparatuses, most notably the Panopticon. It is a practice that
encompasses a complex array of elements that merge the material and the discursive. But Barad also faults Foucault for failing to fully describe the inseparability of observing apparatuses and observed (2007:201). For Barad this inseparability is central. Intra-action, unlike interaction, does not presuppose the
prior existence of independent entities.

For Barad this all comes together in her concept of the "phenomenon."
Reality, she claims, is composed of "things-in-phenomena" (2007:140); the primary ontological units of the world are not things but phenomena. Phenomena
are constituted through the intra-action between the observer (plus the apparatus of observation) and the object. They enact the ontological inseparability of
objects and apparatuses: "A phenomenon is a specific intra-action of an 'object'
and the 'measuring agent'" (128). Phenomena are not given, but neither are they
discursively constructed; the primary semiotic events are not words but material/
discursive practices. Discursive practices, furthermore, do not just describe, they
produce:

> On an agential/realist account, *discursive practices are specific material (re)config-
> uring of the world through which local determinations of boundaries, properties and
> meanings are differentially enacted.* That is, *discursive practices are on-going agen-
> tial intra-action of the world* through which local determinacy is enacted within
> the phenomena produced. (148–49)

Barad's intention to provide a counter—a ballast—to linguistic constructionism is most clearly revealed in her critique of Judith Butler. Butler's position
on gender and materiality is, for Barad as well as for the feminist community,
the definitive statement of the position, the gold standard as it were. In "Getting
Real"[7] Barad first takes on Butler, arguing that her theory of materialization
does not go beyond the active/passive dualism. Butler's account of materialization, she argues, is attentive only to the discursive and thus re-inscribes the dualism. As a result "Questions about the material nature of discursive practices
seem to hang in the air like the persistent smile the Cheshire cat" (2007:64). In

a particularly pointed critique, Barad asks, "If it has taken this much to wake us from our ontological illusions, does any reference to material constraint threaten to undercut this achievement?" (192). But Barad's critique is not wholly negative. Rather, her point is to ask whether it is possible to construct a revised account of performativity that would lead us to a realist understanding of the materialization of bodies, one that takes full account of materiality yet does not reinstate it as an uncontested ground.

Barad constructs just such an account of performativity in "Agential Realism: How Discursive Practices Matter."[8] Her central claim is that Butler theorizes performativity only in terms of how discourse comes to matter but fails to analyze how matter comes to matter. It is this oversight that Barad seeks to address. It is significant that, in her effort to formulate a new approach, Barad retains Butler's concept of "performativity" rather than rejecting the concept as inherently flawed. Her retention of the concept, however, is consistent with her theoretical commitment to practice as material/discursive. Barad's goal here is to formulate a *materialist* theory of performativity that, while not denying the role of discourse that Butler emphasizes, also does not deny the role of the material. In contrast to Butler's concept, Barad's agential realist elaboration of performativity allows matter its due as an active participant in the world's becoming (2007:136).

Barad defines her position on performativity as an alternative to the representationalist separation of the world into the ontologically distinct domains of words and things (2007:137)). She contrasts her position on this issue not only to that of Butler but also to that of Foucault. Against Foucault she argues that we need to explain not only how the body is discursively constituted but also how the discursive construction is related to the non-discursive. Her claim is that agential realism can accomplish this goal by acknowledging nature, the body, and materiality in the fullness of their becoming without resorting to the transparency of nature. Thus what we are left with in Barad's account is not a world of words and things that we are trying, ultimately unsuccessfully, to represent—the dilemma of representationalism—but a world of phenomena, of material/discursive practices. The advantages of this position are multiple. First, it removes us from the dead end of representationalism, the futile attempt to "get it right" in terms of representing nature. Second, it brings ontology back into the equation. For Barad, there is something there that we, both scientists and everyday human beings, are interacting or "intra-acting" with. And if there is something there, then we can take the empirical world seriously again. Scientists can study it and we can live in it.

Another advantage of agential realism is particularly significant from a political perspective. Barad argues that material/discursive practices have consequences, consequences that matter to us both as scientists and as human beings living in the world. This would seem to be an obvious fact, but as Barad continually reminds us, it has become less than obvious in the theoretical world of linguistic constructionism. If theory has been reduced to unconstrained play, then the material dimension of theoretical practice is obscured.[9] If what we do as theorists is a game, then which discourse we choose is of no consequence. It is merely one of perhaps an infinite number of options that are equally possible. The thrust of Barad's theory is to counter this tendency. She argues:

> Which material-discursive practices are enacted matters for ontological as well as epistemological reasons: a different material-discursive apparatus materializes a different agential reality, as opposed to simply producing a different description of a fixed observation-independent world. (2001:236)

In "Getting Real: Technoscientific Practices and the Materialization of Reality," Barad analyzes the use of the sonogram to observe fetal development. Barad's analysis here, more than any other aspect of her work, illustrates the theoretical power of her description of a material/discursive practice. The complex array of elements that Barad synthesizes in this analysis reveals both the brilliance of her approach and its comprehensive scope. She states the premise of this approach at the outset: we are responsible for the world in which we live because it is a product of particular practices that we have a role in shaping (2007:203). The practice that she focuses on to illustrate this principle, the use of the sonogram to view the fetus at an early stage of its development, not only reveals the multiple elements of this practice but examines their intra-action in a practice that matters on multiple levels.

Several elements jointly constitute the practice of fetal imaging. The first is technological. Sonograms are instruments, apparatuses that came to be applied in medicine for specific purposes. Apparatuses like the sonogram structure our perception of the real, defining reality in a specific way. Another element is scientific/medical. Developments in medicine made it feasible to "see" the fetus and analyze its condition. These developments also made it possible, in some cases, to alter the condition of the fetus even within the womb. The discursive element adds another dimension. What the "fetus" *is* is an important element in the practice of using sonograms to "see" fetuses. How we define the fetus is structured not only by scientific/medical and technological practice but also by politics. The identity of the fetus is produced by the intra-action of all these elements, not the least of which is the political forces that assign a particular identity to the fetus.

Analyzing the practice of fetal imaging through the lens of agential realism, Barad comes to some startling conclusions. Her first is that specific aspects of matter become agentic through the intra-action of the material-discursive practice of analyzing the fetus with ultrasound. Specifically, the material arrangements of fetal imaging facilitate and are in part conditioned by a political discourse insisting on the autonomy and subjectivity of the fetus. In other words, the "fetus" that the scientist sees through the sonogram, the objective object of the scientific gaze, is the "fetus" that the law has defined as a free-floating subject. In making this statement, Barad exposes the myth of scientific objectivity. But she does more than that. She shows that the scientific/technical and political intra-act. We cannot "see" the fetus in the sonogram without "seeing" it as an autonomous subject under the law.

Barad concludes that the "fetus" is not a preexisting object of investigation with inherent properties but a phenomenon constituted and reconstituted out of historically and culturally situated intra-actions of material-discursive apparatus of bodily production (2007:217).[10] Like Tuana's examination of Katrina, Barad's analysis brings together multiple elements from distinct realms to describe a particular phenomenon. What makes both of these analyses unique is what Barad calls the intra-action of these elements. In commenting on Barad's work, Rouse (2004:155) argues that the importance of her approach is that she not only shows the relation of power to scientific practice—a staple of science studies—but she also shows how to recognize and account for these dimensions of scientific practice without reducing or subordinating scientific knowledge to predetermined structures of power.

What is uniquely powerful about Barad's analysis here is her insight that the scientist/technician cannot "see" the fetus on the screen of the sonogram without at the same time "seeing" it as an autonomous identity. Thus the political enables the technical. Conversely, the political identity of the fetus could not be conceived without the development of the technological/scientific practice of "seeing" the fetus on the sonogram screen. These two "seeings" cannot be neatly separated. They are, in Pickering's sense, part of the mangle. Barad's analysis goes a long way toward revealing how the mangle operates. Her theory gives us a model that can be applied to the constitution of all our cultural practices.[11]

It is my contention that Barad's theory moves beyond that of other philosophers of science by linking two key concepts: objectivity and responsibility. Objectivity, on her account, cannot rest on the separability of elements; such separability is untenable. But it does not follow that objectivity has no ontological component. Rather, objectivity is based in an intra-actively enacted agential separability, a relation of exteriority within phenomena. Thus "Objectivity is about being accountable and responsible to what is real" (2007:340). This link between objectivity and responsibility is of paramount importance:

> On my agential realist account, scientific practices do not reveal what is already there; rather, what is "disclosed" is the effect of the intra-active engagements of our participation within and as a part of the world's differential becoming. (361)

This position, finally, reveals the fundamental error of linguistic constructionism, an error that also foregrounded her discussion of the sonogram:

> We are responsible for the world of which we are a part, not because it is an arbitrary construction of our choosing but because reality is sedimented out of particular practices that we have a role in shaping and through which we are shaped. (390)

This is perhaps the most succinct statement of Barad's position and its implications for both scientific and political practice. It is what gives her theory a unique advantage in the ongoing discussion about what I am calling the new settlement. The last sentence of her book reiterates this forcefully: "We need to meet the universe halfway, to take responsibility for the role that we play in the world's differential becoming" (396).[12]

In *How Scientific Practices Matter* Joseph Rouse argues that feminist science studies are moving toward a "postepistemological" conception of knowledge, evidence, justification, and objectivity (2002:146). This claim is amply substantiated in a special issue of *Feminist Theory* in 2004 devoted to what the authors call the "new materialism." Myra Hird defines the new materialism as marking "a momentous shift in the natural sciences in the past few decades to suggest an openness and play within the living *and* non-living world, contesting previous paradigms which posited a changeable culture against a stable and inert nature" (2004:2). Like Tuana and Barad, the new materialists want to demonstrate how the new approach works in practice, how it makes a difference. The authors collected in the special issue do this through analyses of how this "openness and play" operates in science studies and feminist theory. Hird's book *Sex, Gender, and Science* (2004) puts the new materialism to work in an analysis of how society and science have structured the concept of "sex" to emphasize differences rather than similarity. Together the work of the new materialists demonstrate the differences entailed by defining materiality as both active and positive.[13]

Tuana's "interaction" and "viscous porosity," Barad's "intra-action" and "agential realism," and the "new materialism" of feminist science studies are, indeed, as Rouse claims, beginning to transform feminist approaches to knowledge. This transformation is evident in the feminist science studies cited above, but it has also made deep inroads into an area that has always been central to feminist analysis: the body. For feminism, the body is unavoidable, but it is also problematic. Women's bodies are the point of intersection between patriarchal structures and women's lives. It is women's bodies that feel the pain those structures create, and it is also women's bodies that have been constructed as the cause of women's inferiority. Dealing with women's bodies has thus always been a necessary aspect of feminist analysis but also one of the most difficult.

With the advent of linguistic constructionism in feminist theory, however, the body became problematic in an entirely new way. Judith Butler's *Bodies That Matter* (1993) released a firestorm of critique that brought the status of the body in feminist theory after postmodernism to the forefront. Critics of Butler have attacked her from many directions, but one critique stands out: the claim that despite the aspiration of postmodernism to deconstruct dichotomies, Butler's approach to the body in effect reifies the modernist dichotomy of the body as either a brute given or a representational effect (Bray and Colebrook 1998:42). Feminists expressed widespread discontent with what they saw as Butler's privileging of discourse over materiality in her analysis of the body. Yet precisely how to avoid this theoretical stance remained unclear.

Susan Bordo has been both a consistent defender of the materiality of the body and a critic of the strictly linguistic approach to the body attributed to Butler.[14] But Bordo's position is far from a simplistic materialism. Instead, in works like *Unbearable Weight* (1993) her analyses of anorexia and bulimia as "cultural diseases" merge culture, nature, and biology into an indistinguishable mix. In recent years the attempt to find an alternative to linguistic constructionism, an attempt that picks up many of the themes of Bordo's work, has fueled a new approach to the body that radically alters the terms of the debate. Many feminists are now arguing that we should not be forced to choose between discourse and materiality, culture and nature. Rather, we should devise an approach to the body that overcomes these dualisms, that defines the body as a "complex and dynamic configuration of events that includes the material and the corporeal" (Bray and Colebrook 1998:44). Proponents of this approach define the body as a "transformer," a complex interlay of highly constructed social and symbolic forces (Braidotti 2002:20–22). This approach, they argue, constitutes a "healthy and exciting new era in feminist philosophy" (Kukla 2006:vii).

The feminist theorist who is most closely associated with this new approach to the body is Elizabeth Grosz. Her 1994 book, *Volatile Bodies*, stakes out what is at issue very clearly. At the outset Grosz states that we need to think about bodies in a non-dualistic way, to displace the centrality of mind in discussions of the subject and make the subject a corporeal being. But it is not enough only to avoid the dualisms that have defined the body in Western thought; we also need to avoid essentialism. Grosz argues that the means to accomplish this is to re-think one of the pillars of feminist thought: the sex/gender distinction: "Gender is not an ideological superstructure added to a biological base" (1994:58). Grosz's argument is that unless we can transcend this dichotomy that has grounded so much feminist thought, we will not be able to transform our approach to the body.

One of Grosz's most effective means of addressing this issue is her argu-ment that masculine and feminine gender cannot be neutrally attributed to bodies of either sex. Theorists of the sex/gender distinction defined bodies as blank slates on which gender is inscribed. Grosz counters this with the point that the same message inscribed on a male or female body does not have the same meaning (1994:156). Her argument is that bodies matter, but they are not the only thing that matters. Like the other feminist theorists of the new materi-alism, Grosz is trying to include the material without excluding the discursive. Subjectivity, she asserts, is fully material, but it is a materiality extended to in-clude the operations of language, desire, and signification (210).

Grosz elaborates on these themes in *Space, Time, and Perversion: Essays on the Politics of Bodies* (1995). The specific object of her critique here is the effects of linguistic constructionism on discussions of the body. Her contention is that after Butler's *Gender Trouble* the dominant trend in feminist theory has been to focus on discourse at the expense of bodies. Bodies entail biologism and essen-tialism, the traps of modernism. Grosz wants to reverse this by providing a non-biologistic, nonreductive account of the body. She boldly asserts that sexual dif-ference is the ontological condition of human bodies. Human bodies are always sexed bodies. But this is not all there is to the story. The sex assigned to a body has a great deal to do with the kind of social subject the body will be (1995:85). The body, Grosz concludes, is incomplete: "It is indeterminate, amorphous, a series of uncoordinated potentialities that require social triggering, ordering, and long-term 'administration'" (104).

Grosz's attempt to approach the body in radically different terms is echoed in the work of other contemporary feminist theorists. Like Grosz, Moira Gatens emphasizes sexual difference, challenging the neutrality of the body implicit in much gender theory. The connection between femininity and the female body, masculinity and the male body, she asserts, is not arbitrary (1996:4). There are two kinds of bodies: male and female. Her thesis is that the same behavior will have different significance when acted out by male or female bodies (8–9). In order to formulate her alternative approach to the body, Gatens turns to the work of Spinoza. Unlike other theorists in the Western tradition, Spinoza presents a non-dualistic philosophy in which the body is the ground of human action. Building on Spinoza's work, Gatens develops a conception of the body that focuses on what Barad would call the intra-action of bodies and culture. For Gatens bodies exist, but what they are at any given time is always historical and cultural: "Past contingencies become the material of present necessities" (103). Bodies are always in interconnection with other body complexes. Gatens concludes that it is only within these complex assemblages that sexed bodies are produced as socially and politically meaningful bodies (149).

What the new feminist theorists of the body have accomplished constitutes a new era in feminist theory: an ontology of the body. The emphasis of these theories is that bodies *exist*, but they exist in intra-action with a complex array of forces (Colebrook 2000). Grosz's and Gatens's explorations of this ontology stay almost exclusively within the realm of theory. Other feminists exploring the ontology of the body, however, have moved their analyses into the real world that bodies inhabit. A good example of this is Annemarie Mol's analysis in *The Body Multiple: Ontology in Medical Practice* (2002). Mol calls her approach "ontological politics," a position based on the assumption that the conditions of possibility (the real) are not given but enacted (1999:75). In her book, Mol examines how medicine "enacts" the objects of its concern and treatment, how it creates an ontological politics. Instead of focusing on objects in her analysis, Mol focuses on practices. Her thesis is that objects are "enacted" in practices; they come into being and disappear in the practices within which they are manipulated (2002:5).

For Mol reality multiplies along with objects; the two are linked in the practices in which they exist. Unlike previous science studies, Mol's focus is ontological not epistemological. But her ontology is not given in the order of things. It is instead brought into being through practices. The specific subject of Mol's analysis is atherosclerosis. She analyzes the treatment and experience of this disease from the perspective of doctors, patients, relatives of patients, and others in the health care system. But Mol is careful to distinguish her approach from perspectival interpretation. Unlike a perspectival approach, Mol's analysis foregrounds practices, materialities, events. In practices, objects are enacted. The result is what she calls "ontology-in-practice." The theoretical significance of her work, Mol hopes, is to shift the understanding of objects as the focus of various perspectives to following them as they are enacted in a variety of practices. Her question is not how science represents, but how it intervenes (2002:152).

Mol's book is a striking illustration of how the shift to ontology alters the theoretical landscape of feminism. Mol is very clear in her rejection of epistemology and representationalism. For Mol knowledge is no longer primarily referential but a practice that interferes with other practices (2002:153). But she is also clear that the shift to ontology does not entail a return to modernity: "If practice becomes our entrance into the world, ontology is no longer a monist whole. Ontology-in-practice is multiple" (157). Different enactments of, in this case, a disease, entail different ontologies. Mol's goal is to analyze modes of coordination, distribution, and inclusion that allow different versions of a single object to exist (180). For Mol everything is continually in flux, but it is a flux that is grounded in real bodies, a real disease, and real lives. Mol's analysis illustrates how what we might call the "new ontology" gives us a new way to understand knowledge and the world.[15]

Elizabeth Grosz summarizes the significance of feminists' new approach to the body in *The Nick of Time*: "If the body is to be placed at the center of political theory and struggle, then we need to rethink the terms in which the body is understood" (2004:3). With this statement Grosz introduces another aspect of the new materialism that feminists are developing. For Grosz the new terms in which the body should be understood can only be formulated by addressing an issue that has been off-limits in feminist theory since the rise of linguistic constructionism: biology. Grosz sets out to transgress these limits. The goal of *The Nick of Time* is to explore how the biological prefigures and makes possible the various permutations of life that constitute natural, social, and cultural existence (2004:1). As Grosz is well aware, feminism's relationship to biology is highly problematic. Biological essentialism has been identified as one of the root causes of sexism from the advent of feminism. Thus, approaching this subject is fraught with multiple dangers. But it is Grosz's contention that we must bring biology back into feminist theory if we are to develop the political critiques that feminism needs to further its cause.

What Grosz proposes is an understanding of biology that enables rather than limits. Biology, she asserts, is a system of differences that engenders historical, cultural, social, and sexual differences. It does not limit social, political, and personal life, but makes them possible (2004:1). In order to elaborate her conception of the relationship between nature and culture, Grosz turns to a theorist who has been anathema to feminists because of his alleged biological determinism: Darwin. Grosz's interpretation of Darwin contests this characterization. For Grosz, Darwin's understanding of the relationship between culture and nature is that "culture produces the nature it needs to justify itself, but nature is also that which resists by opening according to its own logic and procedures" (72).

Grosz's purpose, however, is much more than a reinterpretation of Darwin. She wants feminism to embrace what she calls "a politics of affirmation of difference" (2004:72). Central to that goal is a reconfiguration of nature as dynamic, of matter as culturally productive. Grosz sees Darwin's work as facilitating rather than hindering her project. Along with the other new materialists, she is arguing that we need a new way of knowing that focuses on ontology rather than epistemology, the real rather than the production of knowledge (18). These themes carry over into Grosz's next book, appropriately titled *Time Travels* (2005). Here her attempt is to elaborate on the new conception of ontology that she sketched in the previous book. Again, she looks to Darwin. Darwin's "ontology," she claims, defines life and matter as the two orientations in the universe. What we can learn from Darwin is that human practices such as language are never adequate to life and matter. They try to contain them, but they always and necessarily escape (2005:40–42).

Even though Grosz does not mention Pickering's mangle in her analysis, there are significant similarities between the two theories. Like Pickering, Grosz emphasizes the resistance of nature. She asserts that it is the resistance of the world to human wishes, its capacity to make us want, that makes us produce and invent (2005:128). Grosz characterizes this resistance in her discussion of "things." The thing is the point of intersection between space and time, the localization of materiality. Like Barad's phenomena, things do not have an objective existence in the world; the thing is what we make of the world, not what we find in the world (33). Grosz joins Pickering, Latour, Barad, and Tuana in presenting a theory of dynamic intra-action between culture and nature that privileges neither side of the dichotomy.

Another theorist who begins with a consideration of feminist approaches to the body and moves on to an exploration of the broader framework of such analyses is Elizabeth Wilson. Wilson's premise is that, despite intensive scrutiny of the body in recent feminist literature, certain fundamental aspects of the body, specifically biology and materiality, have been foreclosed (1999:16). Like Grosz, Wilson believes that this foreclosure has both theoretical and political consequences: "Critiques premised on a primarily oppositional relation to the sciences or premised on antibiologism, antiessentialism or antirationalism are losing their critical and political purchase" (1998:200). While Grosz turns to biology, and particularly the biology of Darwin, to make her point, Wilson turns to neurology. A feminist analysis of neuropsychology, she claims, will enable feminist psychology to rethink the nature of feminist psychology and the politics of feminist intervention in general (67). In order to accomplish this Wilson turns to what might seem a curious theoretical source: Derridean deconstruction. Wilson uses Derrida to examine psychology as a science under erasure, a science radically at odds with the binaries that seek to control it (88). But despite this significantly different strategy, Wilson ends up occupying the same theoretical space as Grosz. She concludes that the feminist emphasis on gender has meant that the possibility of thinking biology as "other than an excluded, distant, and foundational use has been foreclosed in the majority of feminist projects" (54).

~~~

The attempt to avoid the dualism of nature and culture, essentialism and social construction is not unique to the thinkers discussed here. Vicki Kirby's *Telling Flesh* (1997) is an extended analysis of this dualism and the attempt to overcome it. Toril Moi (1999) turns to one of the foremothers of feminism, Simone de Beauvoir, to argue for a new understanding of the biological basis of feminine existence. I noted earlier that Nelson and Wylie claim that feminist science studies are carving out an alternative to objectivism on one hand and social construction on the other. The works of Grosz, Wilson, Kirby, Moi, and others indicate that feminists in many different fields are also seeking such an alternative. I am not claiming, however, that the new materialism or intra-actionism of these thinkers is the dominant paradigm in feminism today. Clearly, linguistic constructionism still holds sway in many areas of feminist thought. What I am claiming is that, in Kirby's words, "some reassessment needs to be made regarding the implications of exchanging nature for culture, reality for representation, and originary cause for interpretive effect" (1997:150). A sea change in feminism and critical theory is under way that is in the process of altering our fundamental understandings of the relationship between knowledge and the world.

What I have tried to accomplish in this chapter is, first, to outline the parameters of the feminist settlement and, second, to present an argument for the advantages of that settlement. My contention is that the feminist settlement, because it moves beyond the theoretical to the real world implications of the approach, provides a better understanding of the settlement. But it should be obvious even from this overview that much work remains to be done. The parameters of the feminist settlement, despite the careful work of the theorists described here, are still vague. Furthermore, some aspects of the settlement, most notably the analysis of science, are more developed than others. Finally, there is a glaring omission in these accounts that should be especially significant for feminists: few theorists discuss the implications of this approach for the social world. Although Tuana, Barad, and some of the other theorists discussed here have begun the difficult work of extending the approach to the social realm, the task is far from complete. But if this approach is to fulfill its potential to offer a transformed view of knowledge and the world, it must move beyond the confines of science. Most particularly, because it is a feminist approach, it must encompass the social as well as the scientific.

Approaching the social from the perspective provided by these feminist theorists is the task of the next chapter. My goal is to explore the question of a social ontology. This project is crucially important for a number of reasons. First, feminism is necessarily a social theory. It is concerned with women as embodied humans living a social existence. If this new approach is to transform not only feminism but critical thought more broadly, it must necessarily include a social ontology. Second, ignoring the parameters of a specifically social ontology while exploring ontology in nature and science once more reifies the nature/culture dichotomy that is at the heart of modernity. If we are to overcome this dichotomy, we must bring ontology into the realm of the social as well as the natural. We cannot be content with a theory that restricts ontology to the natural world while defining the social as the realm of linguistic construction. Unless we can deconstruct this dichotomy as well, our task will remain incomplete.

5

FROM CONSTRUCTION
TO DISCLOSURE

Ontology and the Social

In "What is Enlightenment?" (1984) Foucault tries to describe in precise terms what he calls the "ethos" of his critical work. Foucault's reference to the Enlightenment in the title of this article is curious. His work is usually identified as challenging the fundamental principles of the Enlightenment, yet here he is arguing for a connection to that tradition. His thesis is that we are historically determined by the Enlightenment; it is, in a sense, who we are. But he then goes on to argue for a more positive and personal connection to the Enlightenment. He asserts that the kind of critical analysis he engages in is a continuation of the ethos of the Enlightenment. It is worth looking again at this key passage:

> The critical ontology of ourselves has to be considered not, certainly, as a theory, a doctrine, nor even as a permanent body of knowledge that is accumulating; it has to be conceived as an attitude, an ethos, a philosophical life in which the critique of what we are is at one and the same time the historical analysis of the limits

that are imposed on us and an experiment in the possibility of going beyond them. (1984:50)

For Foucault there is both continuity and difference in his relationship with the Enlightenment. Like Enlightenment thinkers he is engaged in an analysis of who we are and how we came to be, a "historical ontology of ourselves" (45). But he has broken with the Enlightenment's search for a doctrine, a "permanent body of knowledge":

> Criticism is no longer going to be practical in the search for formal structures with universal value, but rather as a historical investigation into the events that have lead us to constitute ourselves and to recognize ourselves as subjects of what we are doing, thinking, and saying. (46)

In this context Foucault does not give us much indication of what this historical ontology of ourselves would look like. But there are some hints. It will be a "historico-practical test of the limits that we may go beyond." It must address these questions: How are we constituted as subjects of our own knowledge? How are we constituted as subjects who exercise and submit to power relations? (1984:47–49).

In chapter 3 I argued that Foucault's work provides a settlement to the problems posed by modernity. My thesis is that Foucault successfully deconstructs the dichotomies that constitute modernity, offering an understanding of material/discursive practices that privileges neither the discursive nor the material. I now want to take Foucault's work in another direction—to explore the possibility of an ontology of the social world. What Foucault suggests here and practices throughout his work is that what we *are*, our material existence in the social world, is constituted by the boundaries and limits of that world. That we *are*, that we exist as bodies in space, is never an issue for Foucault. What we need to figure out is how that bodily existence comes into being in the confines of our specific social world. We need to understand, first, the events that have led us to constitute ourselves in such a way and, second, precisely what it is that we recognize *as* a subject. Although Foucault is not concerned exclusively with subjects in his exploration of what I am calling social ontology, it is clear that for him the subject is at the center of the social world. It is and must be the beginning of our understanding of that world.

Before engaging in this analysis, however, I must treat two preliminary issues. The first is ontology. In the preceding chapters I have argued that a crucial, if not *the* crucial, aspect of the settlements I am discussing here is the move from epistemology to ontology. What this move entails for the natural sciences is at this point fairly clear. Latour, Pickering, Tuana, and Barad all argue that the world constrains our concepts of it, that the relationship between material and discursive is, in Barad's terms, an intra-action that privileges neither element. We are, in Pickering's sense, always in the mangle. Language does not constitute the world or mirror its reality. The "new ontology" of these thinkers rejects both the fixed ontology of modernity and the linguistic constructionism of postmodernism.

The question I want to address in this chapter is how to bring this new ontology into the social realm. Several difficulties immediately present themselves. It is very tempting to argue that although the natural world possesses a reality that we must take into account, that it "punches back" at us, this is not true of the social world. It seems abundantly obvious that unlike the natural world the social world is entirely constituted by our concepts. Subjects, institutions, practices, and every other aspect of the social world are what they are because of the concepts we use to describe them. Their materiality seems to be entirely a function of our discourse. The problem with this argument from the perspective I am articulating here, however, is that it once more falls into the trap of dichotomous thinking. If we in a sense give up on the ontology of the social, we are in effect reifying the nature/culture dichotomy. Unless we can grapple with the reality of social entities, we will not be able to complete the task of articulating a new settlement.

The feminist theorists discussed in the previous chapter have made significant progress toward revealing how the natural world and its reality participate in the constitution of many aspects of the social. Tuana's discussion of Katrina and Barad's examination of the sonogram are excellent examples of this. The feminist theorists of the body have also illustrated this very effectively. But this is only one aspect of the social ontology. We need to explore the full dimensions of the mangle that constitutes social life. We need to explore the ontology of social institutions such as politics, the economy, religion, kinship. These institutions are in a sense purely social. They have no "natural" component; they would not exist outside our conceptions of them. Yet they are at the same time real. Their existence produces material consequences for the subjects who inhabit the societies they constitute.

Contemporary social and political theorists have made little headway in the exploration of an ontology of the social. In *The Ethos of Pluralization* (1995) William Connolly expresses regret that the ontological dimension of political life is rarely discussed. Although he makes it clear that he rejects the fixed ontology of modernity, Connolly nevertheless wants to assert that every political interpretation presupposes a set of what he calls "fundaments" about the necessities and possibilities of human being (1995:1). But Connolly's goal is not to detail what he calls this "ontopolitical dimension," but rather to define a "more generous pluralism," one that draws contending ontopolitical dispositions into an "enlarged network of intersections" (28). Connolly labels his strategy "ontopolitical interpretation," a strategy that projects ontopolitical presumptions explicitly on detailed interpretations of actuality while acknowledging that the truth of any of these presuppositions cannot be established (36).

The theorists of the new ontology emphasize that ontology is always in flux, that is, that the reality we disclose through our material/discursive practices is fluid rather than fixed. Connolly embraces this position but takes it to an extreme. His concern is almost exclusively with the flux of ontology. His goal, he claims, is pluralization with pluralism, "multiple lines of division that do not correspond to one another on the same plane" (1995:178). Critical pluralism, he concludes, "honors politics as the multifaceted medium through which the multiple dissonances within it are exposed and negotiated" (198). The problem with Connolly's approach here is a matter of balance and emphasis. The new ontology encompasses both reality and flux: reality is in flux, but there *is* reality. Connolly's approach puts so much emphasis on flux that reality is obscured. His concern is to keep everything fluid, to continually expose and negotiate the ontopolitical. The danger of this approach, however, is that it is all too easy to forget that there is a political, material reality that is there to be exposed and negotiated. We need a theory that can explore and acknowledge this reality and its material effects.

Stephen White's account of a political ontology is more robust. White begins *Sustaining Affirmation: The Strengths of Weak Ontology in Political Theory* (2000) by claiming that there is a trend in recent political theory toward ontology. White argues for what he calls "weak ontology," a position that rejects the strong ontology of modernity on one hand and relativism on the other. Weak ontology is an interpretation of being that is not provisional or thin but deeply affirmed and rich, yet one that is contestable (2000:114). White puts less emphasis than does Connolly on the flux of ontology. But like Connolly, his discussion of ontology comes across as tentative; he is unwilling to actively address the reality that his ontology presupposes. The characterization of his ontology as "weak" is, in the end, appropriate.

Acknowledging and exploring social/political reality, however, is precisely what an ontology of the social must accomplish. We must be able to account for the material reality of our social existence without losing sight of the discursive dimension of that reality. As both Foucault and Barad remind us, theories, discourses, have material consequences. The social/political world in which we live is all too real. In our zeal to keep things continually in flux, we must not lose sight of that reality. We must develop tools to examine the parameters of that reality, a reality that, although fluid, structures the world that we as social subjects inhabit.

A second preliminary issue is one that I mentioned briefly in the foregoing: disclosure. It is my contention that the concept of disclosure is just such a tool; that is, it best captures the relationship between knowledge and the world that emerges from the new settlements. Disclosure navigates the gap between constitution on one hand and the brute given on the other. It avoids the problems of representationalism and emphasizes the ontological character of knowing.

In *How Scientific Practices Matter* (2002) Joseph Rouse utilizes the concept of disclosure to describe his understanding of how scientific practices operate. He argues that the natural world is *disclosed* through scientific interaction. Science *discloses* a world for us; it does not appeal to a given concept of nature. We are located in the midst of scientific and technological practices that continue to reshape what it is to be nature (2002:360). One of the most useful aspects of Rouse's concept from my perspective is his rejection of the natural/social science divide. He emphasizes that people interact within a shared environment, that environment can be the purview of the natural or the social sciences. It is not the case that certain kinds of objects—those studied by the natural sciences, for example—are intrinsically meaningful. Rather, meaningfulness emerges as a product of people interacting in a shared environment; it is the situated disclosure of anything as what it is. This disclosure can occur only within ongoing patterns of practical interaction. In sum, he asserts, it is a configuration of the world as intelligible (133).

Rouse does not go beyond these brief comments in his discussion of disclosure. However, I would like to significantly expand this concept and use it as a foundation for the new understanding of the knowledge/world connection I am trying to articulate. Unlike "construction," disclosure presupposes an external reality that is the object of discursive practices. But the external reality presupposed is not fixed. Rather, it is a product of agents' interaction in a shared environment with a world that emerges through that interaction. It is an intra-action between knowledge and the world, not a one-way movement either from the world to our concepts (mirroring) or a projection from the discursive realm onto the world (construction).

I need to be clear about the understanding of "disclosure" I am employing in this context. There are two definitions of disclosure that I want to reject. One is the definition of disclosure as "to uncover, to expose to view" (OED). This understanding of disclosure comes dangerously close to modernity. It entails that we are "getting it right" in an objectivist sense, revealing the one true reality. I also want to reject Heidegger's understanding of the concept. For Heidegger disclosure has a mystical component—the showing forth of Being throughout the ages. In contrast, my understanding of disclosure is very grounded and practical. It is an expression of, in Wittgenstein's sense, the human form of life.

The definition of disclosure that I want to embrace is the intransitive definition: "to show itself, to come to light" (OED). On this definition disclosure does not entail uncovering, getting reality right, but bringing it to light. Different aspects of reality can be disclosed from different perspectives. One of these aspects is not right and the others wrong; rather, they represent different aspects of the same reality. But importantly, it is possible to compare the material consequences of the different disclosures of the same reality. It is my contention that the materiality of disclosure supplies a needed dimension to our understanding of the interaction between knowledge and the world.

Disclosure is not a refutation of relativism or skepticism but a new way of approaching the issues of knowledge and reality. It avoids the problems of representationalism by offering another way of understanding the relationship between language and reality. Disclosure entails that perspectives/concepts/theories matter—that they are our means of accessing reality. But disclosure also entails that we do not constitute that reality with our concepts, but rather portray it in varying ways. An important aspect of this understanding is that the reality, like the object in a photograph or the subject of the scientist's experiment, is agentic. It pushes back, it affects the result. Another important aspect of this understanding is that there *is* a result. There are different material consequences to different disclosures. We can compare those material consequences and make arguments about which ones are more useful. We will not convince everyone with these arguments. We cannot appeal to an objective reality to trump the argument. But we have something to argue *about*.

Foucault's work can be interpreted as an instance of disclosure, as I am articulating it here. Foucault reveals that different epistemes disclose different worlds. As those epistemes change, so do the worlds they disclose. But for Foucault this does not result in endless relativism. Foucault's analysis of carceral society is designed to reveal the dire material consequences of this particular disclosure. It is also designed to suggest that under a different episteme we might be different—and better—subjects. His argument is not that we can get it *right* but that a different episteme might result in more favorable material consequences.

Barad's analysis of the use of the sonogram provides another example. The sonogram discloses the "reality" of the "fetus," but this reality is defined, not by the brute reality of an object in a woman's womb, but by the complex interaction of science, technology, politics, and cultural forces. The result of this complex mix, this mangle, is "seeing" the fetus on the screen of the sonogram. This seeing has consequences not only for the fetus and the mother of the fetus but

for reproductive politics in the wider society. This "seeing" has material consequences that extend far beyond the sonogram screen.[1] It is precisely the character of this mangle in the social/political world that we all inhabit that I wish to
explore.

Disclosures have real material consequences. To disclose is not to reveal the
true objective reality of an object. Rather, it is to engage in a complex practice in
which multiple elements interact, or intra-act, to produce an understanding of
the reality that we share. Disclosure avoids relativism because it gives us something to compare: we can weigh the material consequences of one configuration
over another. In contrast, linguistic constructionism forces us to conclude that
every story is just as valid as any other story. Disclosure gives us another option.
We can argue that certain disclosures have material consequences that are ben-
eficial, others that are not. We still cannot argue for absolute truth. But we can
make arguments grounded in the material consequences of the disclosure we
practice.

Subjects

Any ontology of the social must begin with the issue that is at the same time the
most compelling and the most difficult aspect of social existence: the subject.
Societies are constituted by subjects. What a subject is—or is not—is definitive
of every society. Much of the debate between moderns and postmoderns, furthermore, has revolved around the definition of the subject: is there an essential
"I," or is the subject a fiction, a product of the performance of social scripts, a
social dupe? This question has been hotly debated in recent years, particularly
by feminists. How we define the subject "woman" has been crucial to how we
define feminism and its role in social change.

My goal in developing an ontology of the subject is to navigate through these
dangerous waters, and especially to avoid both extremes in the dispute over the
subject: defining the subject either as wholly a social construct or as a given, essential entity. Instead, I want to use the insights of Pickering, Foucault, Barad,
and others to describe the subject as a mangle, an entity that is discursive *and*
material, natural *and* social, a product of the intra-action of all these forces. I also
want to emphasize the uniqueness of the subject and its vulnerability. As subjects
in a given society, we *live* in the mangle. Its various components constitute our
lives and who we are. Furthermore, through their social practices societies define
who qualifies as a subject, quite literally who can *be*. It follows that the ontology
of the subject is uniquely vulnerable to these practices. Being a subject, a necessary component of a viable life, is dependent on the social scripts available in any

given society. If one falls outside of these scripts, one ceases to have what Butler calls a "livable" life.

The theorist who has laid the groundwork for the description of the subject as a material/discursive product is Michel Foucault. Perhaps more than any other theorist in the twentieth century, Foucault focused attention on the discursive constitution of the subject. His discussion of the constitution of subjects in the modern era—the mentally ill, the criminal, the homosexual—quite literally transformed our conception of subjectivity. But what is frequently overlooked in the discussions of Foucault's revolutionary concept of subjectivity is that he never loses sight of the material dimension of subjectivity. It is the material conditions of prisons, asylums, and hospitals as well as the technological apparatuses that they employ—most notably the panopticon—that structure subjectivity. For Foucault these material/discursive/technological practices that constitute subjectivity create the real conditions of existence for subjects.

The focus of my discussion is the complex relationship between the ontology of the subject—*being* a subject, having an identity—and the power of discursive norms in society. What it comes down to is both simple and immensely complicated. I can only be a subject if my identity conforms to one of the identities offered by the society in which I live. If my identity falls outside the range of acceptable identities, then I quite literally cease to *be*: my ontological existence is erased. This ontological relationship is of unparalleled importance. The social norms establishing identity have the power at the same time to control ontology. In the subject's social existence the relationship between identity and ontology is dangerously intimate.

Ladelle McWhorter articulates this point in her discussion of Foucault and sexual normalization (1999). McWhorter argues that Foucault's genealogical approach affirms the existence of something while at the same time acknowledging its historicity, its inessentiality. Being a lesbian, she declares, is my identity, not my nature (1999:30–31). McWhorter concludes that for Foucault identity is not an essential, natural quality but a social construct to which the individual must conform. Enforcing that conformity, furthermore, is the power society exercises to define who is a subject and who is not. McWhorter argues that she is a lesbian because she conforms to the lesbian identity extant in our society. This has nothing to do with her essential nature. But it is also the case that it is her only option if she wants to be a subject at all.

Foucault's discussion of the hermaphrodite Herculine Barbin (1980a) illustrates this connection between ontology and identity. But, curiously, his interpretation of the story ends up contradicting his theoretical position on sexuality. Throughout his work Foucault consistently maintains that there is no essential "sex," but rather that sex is produced by the complex interaction of discourse and power. Yet in his discussion of the case of Herculine, Foucault appears to deny this point. He asserts that Herculine's sexual pleasure is the result of a "happy limbo of non-identity," implying that this sexual pleasure transcends the social construction of "sex." In her critique of Foucault's analysis, Judith Butler (1990:100) argues that Foucault contradicts himself regarding the status of sexual pleasure in this discussion. Butler is undoubtedly right here. Foucault's theory should lead him to deny the possibility of Herculine's sexual pleasure. But I would draw a different conclusion from Foucault's analysis. Herculine's dilemma was that he/she was denied an identity. He/she was offered two possible identity options: man or woman. No middle ground was available. Accepting neither option did not result in a happy limbo of non-identity but in a decidedly unhappy limbo of nonbeing. Herculine could not *be* because there was no identity option open to him/her that he/she could occupy. The result was, eventually, suicide.[2]

Foucault is very good on the ontology of the subject in one very crucial respect: he explains the intra-action of the material, discursive, and technological in the constitution of the modern subject. But he is less helpful on the question raised by Herculine Barbin: the relationship between the being of the subject and the identity options open to him/her in society. There are some vague references to the possibility of a new economy of bodies and pleasures in his work, but there is no extended discussion of the problem facing Herculine Barbin: what are the options for subjects who are denied identity and hence an ontology?

This is a question, however, that has been of intense concern to feminist thinkers. I argued above that feminists have been at the forefront of the constitution of the emerging settlement. Feminist explorations of the subject, and especially the ontology of the subject, provide further evidence of this claim. Feminists have focused on the question of the subject since de Beauvoir's assertion that women are made, not born. Much effort was expended to define a subject compatible with feminist goals. With the advent of linguistic constructionism, however, the issue of the subject was problematized in a different way. New questions arose: How can we define the subject as a product of discourse without losing the ontology of that subject? How can we account for the fact that women have bodies and pain and live in a real world?

The feminist theorist whose work addresses these questions most productively is Judith Butler. Butler seems an unlikely source for the development of an ontology of the subject. If there is one theorist who stands for the linguistic constructionism that has dominated feminist theory in the last several decades, it is Butler. But I think that, particularly in her recent work, Butler moves beyond linguistic constructionism to something that can be described as an ontology of the subject. There are several reasons for this movement. First, she is a student of Foucault, and, as I have argued, Foucault's work significantly challenges linguistic constructionism. Second, she is acutely interested in the question that Foucault sidesteps: how one can *be* as a subject outside the accepted identity categories of a society. As a result, in her post–*Gender Trouble* work, Butler appears to realize the limitations of a strict linguistic constructionism and move in another direction. Beginning with *The Psychic Life of Power* (1997) a new entity enters Butler's theoretical landscape: a "being" that escapes subjectification:

> We might reread "being" as precisely the potentiality that remains unexhausted by any particular interpellation. Such a failure of interpellation may well undermine the capacity of the subject to "be" in a self-identical sense, but it may also mark the path toward a more open, basic, even more ethical kind of being, one of or for the future. (1997:131)

What I will argue is that Butler, despite her commitment to an inessential subject, is forced by the logic of her argument to explore the possibilities that escape this subject. Her exploration of these possibilities leads in some interesting and unexpected directions (Hekman 2004:15).

The springboard for Butler's consideration of the ontology of the subject comes, not surprisingly, from her analysis of Foucault. The last sentences of Butler's first book, *Subjects of Desire* (1987), set the stage for the considerations that are to follow: "From Hegel through Foucault, it appears that desire makes us into strangely fictive beings. And the laugh of recognition appears to be the occasion of insight" (1987:238). Following Foucault, Butler looks to recognition as the key to the identity of the subject. And the key to recognition is power.

Butler's most extensive discussion of Foucault, power, and the subject is in a unique article first written in 1978, "Bodies and Power Revisited" (2004a). She begins with the assertion that for Foucault, particularly in *Discipline and Punish*, the body is not simply the passive recipient of power. Power happens to the body, but the body is at the same time the occasion in which something happens to power. She goes on to argue that Foucault's concept of power *appears* to be contradictory: if the subject is there to be acted on by power, this would seem to entail that it is prior to power; but if power produces a subject, then power creates the subject. Butler argues, however, that Foucault's position is not contradictory but rather is an important insight into the relationship between power and the subject: "Power attaches a subject to its own identity. Subjects appear to require this self-attachment, this process by which one becomes attached to one's own subjecthood" (2004a:190).

Once more appealing to Foucault, Butler elaborates on her enigmatic reference to the subject who "appears" to require an attachment to subjecthood. She attributes to Foucault the position that every being seeks to persist in its own being, to develop an attachment that will further the cause of its own self-preservation and self-enhancement. But then things get interesting. We are attached to ourselves through mediating norms; norms give back to us a sense of who we are. It follows that one's fundamental attachment to oneself, an attachment without which one cannot *be*, is constrained in advance by social norms. Failure to conform to those norms puts at risk the capacity to sustain a sense of oneself as an enduring subject. She concludes that to challenge the norms by which recognition is conferred is to risk one's being, one's ontology, one's recognizability as a subject (2004a:190–91).

What Butler has accomplished in this early article is to lay out the problem that will concern her, not in *Gender Trouble*, but in the works following this path-breaking book. The problem, simply, is the relationship between the identity of the subject and the ontology of the subject. But if the problem is simple, the solution is not. She confronts this issue in two books, *Undoing Gender* (2004) and *Giving an Account of Oneself* (2005). Taken together, these works might be characterized as representing an ontological turn in Butler's work, a turn away from the linguistic constructionism that marked *Gender Trouble*, and to a lesser extent *Bodies That Matter*, and toward a concern with being.[3] Three themes pervade these books: first, that social norms define what it is to *be* a subject; second, that having an identity, being an "I," is necessary for living a viable life; and, third, that changing the norms that define personhood poses a challenge to society's underlying constitution.

All three themes appear in the first few pages of *Undoing Gender*. Butler begins with a clear statement of the problem: "Sometimes a normative conception of gender can undo one's personhood, undermining the capacity to persevere in a livable life" (2004c:1). Without recognition I cannot live, but the terms by which I am recognized are untenable (4). Certain humans are recognized as less than human and, as a result, denied a viable life. If my options are loathsome, she goes on, then my sense of survival depends on escaping the clutches of these norms:

> If my doing is dependent on what is done to me or, rather, the ways in which I am done in by norms, then the possibility of my persistence as an "I" depends on my being able to do something with what is done with me. (3)

On Butler's reading, then, we are caught in what appears to be an insoluble dilemma. On one hand, "it seems crucial to realize that a livable life does require various degrees of stability" (2004c:8). Yet for some subjects that stability is denied: no viable identity is open to them; they are classified as less-than-human.

The less-than-human, furthermore, are in an impossible situation. They must have an identity to lead a viable life, yet they are denied a viable identity by the social norms that govern them: "For those who are still looking to become possible, possibility is a necessity" (31). Even worse, the only source for the creation of a viable identity is precisely the social norms that deny that possibility. As Butler puts it at the end of the book, norms are what you need to live, but living it will efface you (217).[4]

There is another problem as well: the relationship between the "I" who bears the identity given by norms and the "I" who I am: "I cannot be who I am without drawing on the sociality of norms that precede and exceed me" (2004c:32). And, she asserts, if gender comes from elsewhere, then gender undoes the "I" who is supposed to bear it, and that undoing is part of the very meaning and comprehensibility of that "I" (16). As Butler is well aware, this is dangerous territory. Taken out of context these sentences could be interpreted as implying an essential subject, an "I" who precedes social norms. There is no evidence in the text that this is Butler's intent. She does not pursue this issue further. However, it is an issue that is central to an ontology of the subject. The two options that are open to us—either an essential subject or a wholly socially constructed subject— are both untenable. What we need is something that overcomes this dichotomy, that acknowledges, as Butler does here, the constitutive force of social norms, without denying the "I" on which those norms are projected.

What does concern Butler in the rest of the book is the question of change. The struggle for rights, for her, is the struggle to be conceived as a person. What we need to do, she argues, is to effect a social transformation of the meaning of personhood (2004c:32–33). One of the pillars of gender and identity in contemporary society is kinship relationships. Since identity is defined in many instances in terms of an individual's role in kinship relationships, those who do not fit neatly into these relationships—gays, lesbians, transgendered people, advocates of gay marriage and parenting—are excluded and marginalized. For Butler, challenging the dominance of kinship in constructing gender is the key to "undoing" gender. She points to "postkinship" studies in anthropology that no longer situate kinship as the basis of culture. New kinship and sexual arrangements challenge the relationship between nature and culture. When relations that bind are no longer traced to heterosexual procreation, then the homology between nature and culture compels a rethinking of culture itself (125–28). Her thesis is that expanding the concept of kinship beyond the heterosexual would dislodge the relationship between the biological and the cultural.

What goes for kinship also goes for sexual difference. If we reject the definition of sexual difference as reducible to biology or culture, she asks, how can we understand it ontologically? Her answer is ambiguous: sexual difference registers ontologically in a way that is permanently difficult to determine. Sexual difference is neither fully given nor fully constructed but is partially both. Sexual difference is the site where the question of the relation of the biological and the cultural is posed, but where it cannot be answered (2004c:185–86). One reading of this answer is that Butler is sidestepping this difficult question, in effect refusing to grapple with the complexities of the issue. Another reading, however, is that she is suggesting something akin to Pickering's mangle. The biological and the cultural are not neatly separable. I am not a man or a woman solely because of my genes *or* the social script that defines gender. Rather, the two forces intra-act. As Grosz and Gatens argue, masculinity and femininity in a cultural sense play out differently on male and female bodies.

In *Giving an Account of Oneself* Butler turns to a topic closely related to the identity of the subject: agency, and particularly moral agency. This issue has been the focus of much of the criticism of Butler's work. Many of Butler's critics claim that her conception of the subject obviates agency, turning the subject into a social dupe. Butler's discussion here is in some sense a response to those criticisms. But it is much more than this. After *Gender Trouble*, and to a certain extent *Bodies That Matter*, Butler is less concerned with clarifying the linguistic constructionism of these works than with exploring the ontological implications of identity. This is her concern in this volume.

When the "I" gives an account of itself, Butler begins, it can start with itself, but it will find that it is already interpellated in a social temporality that exceeds its own capacity for narration. The "I" has no strategy of its own that is not also the strategy of a relation to a set of norms. But, Butler asserts, this does not preclude moral agency: "We start to give an account only because we are interpellated as beings who are rendered accountable by a system of justice and punishment" (2005a:10). On the face of it, this passage might seem compatible with Butler's claim in *Gender Trouble* that construction produces agency, that the discursive constitution of the subject is what produces rather than obviates agency. But there is an important change in this text that indicates a significant shift in Butler's thinking. In *Gender Trouble* there is no "I"—the social script is everything. Now we have an "I" who "starts with itself" even if it doesn't end there. This "I" changes everything.

Once more, Butler turns to Foucault, particularly the later work in which Foucault is examining the constitution of the ethical subject.[5] Along with Foucault, she asserts that what I can "be" is constrained by a regime of truth that decides in advance what will and will not be a recognized form of being. But the theme of resistance is there as well: to call into question a regime of truth is to call into question the truth about myself, to question the basis for my own ontological status (2005a:22–23). Thus,

> the "I" is the moment of failure in every narrative effort to give an account of one-self. It remains the unaccounted for and, in a sense, constitutes the failure that the very project of self-narration requires. Every effort to give an account of oneself is bound to encounter this failure and to founder upon it. (79)

That Butler is tentative in these formulations is undoubtedly the case. But it is also the case that her move to ontology is significant. In feminist theory Butler has been the unquestioned source of linguistic constructionism, especially as it relates to the subject. Thus for Butler to turn, even tentatively, to ontology, has important consequences for feminist theory. It seems to indicate that, like Latour, Butler is uncomfortable with the critical path that we have taken and wants to explore an alternative. Butler's work is also significant on another level. Her insightful probings into the constitution of the subject indicate just how difficult the problem is. The depth of those probings reveals that crafting an ontology of the subject will not be easy.

Butler's work reveals that an ontology of the subject must encompass two essential elements. First, it will have to begin with the constitutive function of social norms. These norms tell us what we can be as subjects; they both constrain and empower us. A consequence of the power of social norms is that those excluded from subjecthood are denied a viable life in society. It also follows that attempts to change those norms, to alter what it means to be a subject, will meet with significant resistance. The norms defining the subject are central to what a society is all about. Changing those norms will change the definition of the society itself.

The second element is more difficult: the "I" that is defined by these norms. This "I" is not identical with these norms; it is not wholly created by them. But neither is it an essential subject in the modernist sense. One of the elements of the "I" is a body that has a specific genetic makeup. Social norms play out differently on different bodies. They play out differently as well on the different social locations of those bodies: the social scripts of gender and race, for example, will have a different effect on "I"s located on different levels of the social hierarchy.[6]

What this suggests, then, is that the "I" is a mangle composed of multiple elements. The social scripts defining subjecthood are a key aspect of that mangle. But the mangle also encompasses a body that is sexed and raced, a body that is located at a particular place in the social hierarchy, and a body/subject that has had a range of experiences. The result may be a subject that fits neatly into the definition of subject the social scripts circumscribe. Or the result may be an "I" who cannot find a script that fits, that resists the scripts available to her/him. In all cases, however, there is no single causal factor determining the subject; the elements of subjectivity intra-act in a complex web. In the end, we are left with what appears to be a contradiction: "I am not outside the language that structures me, but neither am I determined by the language that makes this 'I' possible" (Butler 1999:xxiv). But this apparent contradiction is precisely where we must start in our effort to find an ontology of the subject. My contention is that Butler's work has taken us a long way in the direction of developing that ontology.

If Butler's current writings on the subject can be characterized as a turn to ontology, she is not alone. After *Gender Trouble* and *Bodies That Matter* there was an outpouring of criticisms of Butler's theory of identity and the subject (Hekman 2004). In recent years, however, a number of theorists have moved beyond critiques of Butler to the articulation of what they call a "realist" theory of identity. Once more, it is feminists who are the leaders in articulating this theory. The realist theory of identity is concerned with many of the same issues that the "settlements" address. The adherents of the theory attempt to define identity, contra the postmoderns, as a very real part of social life without denying the role of discursive practices in the formation of identity. As such, the realist theorists of identity have made important strides toward the definition of an ontology of the subject.

In 2000 a group of closely connected scholars published *Reclaiming Identity: Realist Theory and the Predicament of Postmodernism* (Moya and Hames-Garcia).[7] The title says it all: the authors' goal is to wrest identity from the grips of postmodern theory and redefine it in a realist direction. The sentiment here is very similar to that expressed by Karen Barad. While Barad wants to construct a ballast against what she defines as the endless play of the postmoderns, the authors of this collection want to rescue identity from the fictive subject of postmodernism. Although they do not cite the authors and concepts discussed here, these authors are moving in a direction very similar to that of the theorists of the new settlements.

The postmodern theory of identity and the related condemnation of identity politics caused difficulties for theorists across the spectrum of intellectual life. But it caused particular difficulties for feminists and scholars of minority studies. If, as the postmoderns claimed, identity is not only a fiction but a fiction imposed by the hegemonic forces of society and thus the cause of the subject's subordination, then those who seek to promote social change should eschew identity. This conclusion, however, is unacceptable to those studying women and racial minorities. If we must eschew identity, how do we characterize the identity of women and minorities? How or can we distinguish these identities from the other identities extant in society? How can we engage in struggles for political change? What, in short, becomes of the foundation of feminism and minority studies: identity politics?

The authors of *Reclaiming Identity* seek to answer these questions. In her introduction to the volume, Paula Moya states that the "postpositivist theory of identity" expressed in the book emerged from the work of a group of scholars in and around Cornell University in the 1990s. Impelling their work were two concerns: opposition to what they saw as the excesses of widespread constructionism and a commitment to progressive politics. These theorists were united around the conviction that any theory of identity is inadequate unless it allows a social theorist to analyze the epistemic status and political salience of any identity and to evaluate the limits and possibilities of different identities. Like the theorists seeking the new settlement discussed here, these theorists are concerned to avoid both sides of the dichotomy of identity established by modernity: identity as either essential or wholly constructed. Against this they argue that identity can be both real and constructed (Moya 2000a).

In her contribution to the volume, Moya states the problem very directly:

> In the current theoretical climate within U.S. literary and cultural studies, the feminist scholar who persists in using categories such as race or gender can be presumptively charged with essentialism, while appeals to "experience" or "identity" may cause her to be dismissed as either dangerously reactionary or hopelessly naïve. (2000b:68)

In the context of a critique of Haraway's concept of identity, and particularly the influential figure of the cyborg, Moya argues for an approach to identity that acknowledges how race, class, gender, and sexuality function in individual lives without reducing individuals to these social determinants (80). What Moya and the other contributors to the volume are attempting to accomplish is to avoid the key problem that has plagued the postmodern concept of identity—the social dupe—without relinquishing the insights gained by the discursive analysis of identity.

At the center of the realist theory of identity that the authors in *Reclaiming Identity* are trying to articulate is the concept of experience. Experience has a bad reputation in postmodern thought. Postmoderns definitively reject experience as an unmediated given. For postmoderns the meaning of experience is always defined by the social location and discursive rules that constitute that location. Thus it can never be a source of knowledge or meaning for the social actor; it is strictly a function of hegemonic discourse. The proponents of the realist theory of identity attempt to rehabilitate the concept of experience, not by returning to the givenness of experience, but by defining experience as the means through which we gain knowledge of the world.

The concept of experience that Moya presents is informed by many postmodern insights but departs from postmodernism by introducing a cognitive component. A postpositivist realist theory of identity, Moya asserts, acknowledges that different social categories together constitute a person's social location and are causally related to the experiences she will have. But this is not all there is to the formulation. It is also the case, Moya argues, that there is a cognitive component to identity that allows for the possibility of error and accuracy in the interpretation of experiences. Our ability to understand fundamental aspects of our world will depend on our ability to acknowledge and understand the social, political, economic, and epistemic consequences of our own social location. For Moya it follows that some identities have greater epistemic value than others (2000b:81–86).

A redefinition of experience also dominates Satya Mohanty's contribution to *Reclaiming Identity* (2000). Experience is foundational to the realist theory of identity, he asserts, not because of its self-evident authenticity but because it provides the raw material of identity. Mohanty's thesis is that personal experience is socially and theoretically constructed, but it is precisely through this mediation that it yields knowledge. Like Moya, Mohanty claims that this allows us to distinguish between accurate and inaccurate interpretations of experience. But he takes this conception a step farther by introducing a definition of objectivity. We can define social and cultural identity, he claims, in terms of "objective social location." It follows that we can identify legitimate vs. illegitimate experience, legitimate vs. spurious identities. For Mohanty this explains how the oppressed may have epistemic privilege: certain social positions produce more reliable knowledge (2000:55–58).[8]

The realist theory of identity expressed in this article is one element of Mohanty's more comprehensive theory, what he calls the "postpositivist conception of objectivity," articulated in his 1997 book *Literary Theory and the Claims of History*. In this wide-ranging work Mohanty takes on all the big issues: objectivity, knowledge, social constructionism, realism, and identity. Despite his considerations of these ambitious and largely abstract topics, however, Mohanty's aim is practical and political. His thesis is that a strong and defensible notion of objectivity best serves progressive cultural and political projects. He argues that the relativism that follows from social constructionism is inadequate to the political goals of progressive groups. He asserts that we need to elaborate a positive but nonidealized conception of the human as well as a minimum conception of rationality (1997:117).

Mohanty's basic presupposition is that all human beings share the practical capacity to understand and evaluate their actions (1997:141). In a pointed attempt to challenge social constructionism, he argues that a thoroughgoing anti-foundationalism does not lead to relativism but to "postpositivist realism":

> Human knowledge is a socially constructed knowledge of the real world; the world exists as an analyzable causal structure and it shapes our knowledge of it. . . . We do not only "discover" reality, we "make" it as well. (193)

What Mohanty is trying to do here, in a very carefully circumscribed manner, is to redefine objectivity and rationality without denying the role of social construction. He is also trying to carve out a space for cross-cultural critique. Common to all persons regardless of culture, he contends, is the capability of acting purposively and evaluating their actions in light of their ideas and previous experiences, of being "rational" (198). This view, Mohanty contends, gives us a way out of relativism and a means of evaluating actions across cultures without denying the evident influence of cultural practices.

There is much that is right about the "postpositivist realist" theory. Their adherents' discontent with the unreconstructed linguistic determinism of most postmodern theory and their attempt to bring politics back into theory, to look at the practical consequences of the theoretical positions we inhabit is cogently argued and persuasive. But I think that these theorists go about their critique in the wrong way. Moya and Mohanty claim to be challenging the realist/anti-realist dichotomy. But in practice they do not succeed in doing so. Their end result is to redefine realism, not to displace the dichotomy. The same is true of the concepts of objectivity and rationality. Although they significantly qualify these concepts, they also argue that we must retain them if we are to formulate a viable theory. Perhaps most significantly, however, postpositivist realists, along with Marxist standpoint theorists, argue that the oppressed have "epistemic privilege," seeing reality more clearly than those in other social locations. This position constitutes a clear instance of representationalism. One of the significant advantages of the settlements discussed above is the rejection of representationalism, the turn from epistemology to ontology. These theorists' claim of epistemic privilege is not consistent with that turn.

The postpositivist realists' emphasis on politics is a significant strength of their approach. They argue that if we want to support political projects to end oppression and domination, we must be able to *say* something about the oppressed without retreating to endless relativism. But there are ways of achieving this goal other than those taken by the postpositivist realists. In her article in *Reclaiming Identity*, Paula Moya argues that social categories of identity have ontological status—real material effects (2000b:87). The implications of this statement provide a better foundation for challenging linguistic constructionism than the path chosen by the postpositivist realists. If theories have real material consequences, then we can compare those consequences, make arguments for the advantage of some of those consequences over others. But we need not move from this to a grounding in the objective, rational, or true. Once more, I think that appealing to the concept of disclosure is useful. Different social locations disclose reality in different ways. We can compare those disclosures and their material effects without arguing for the objectivity or truth of one of them. In other words, we can base our argument on effects rather than objective truth.

The temptation, evident in the postpositivist realist accounts, to fix theory in some objective given reality, is almost overwhelming. It seems obvious that in order to effect political change we should be able to say that this is the way things *really are* with no ambiguity. But it is a temptation we must resist. We can deny the unrestrained relativism of linguistic constructionism more effectively by emphasizing the agentic role of theory. Theories, practices, give agency to particular aspects of reality. These practices have real material effects; they are not arbitrary linguistic constructions. As Barad argues, we are responsible for the world we inhabit. The material effects of that world, furthermore, can be compared. We can weigh the advantages and disadvantages of one over another. But to do so we need not claim the absolute objective truth of one of these perspectives.

Linda Alcoff, along with the other contributors to *Reclaiming Identity*, identifies her position as a realist account of identity. Both in the article in this volume (2000) and in the comprehensive statement of her position in *Visible Identities* (2006), Alcoff elaborates a position that challenges what she calls the "merely linguistic" approach to identity fostered by the postmoderns. But although Alcoff adopts the terminology of the realist position, her approach avoids the pitfalls of that of Moya and Mohanty. She begins her article in the collected volume by identifying the realist account of identity as a perspective in which identities refer outward to objective and causally significant features of the world. Identities, she argues, are not a block to understanding but the location from which we know (2000:315–35). This aspect of her approach seems to be compatible with the realist account of the other contributors. But then Alcoff introduces a significantly different concept, what she calls "ontological pluralism." Realism, she contends, is compatible with ontological pluralism. Ontologies can be thought of a models of reality that capture the world without enjoying a one-to-one correspondence with entities. Ontologies, furthermore, are justified by utility (316).

These statements put Alcoff's reference to objectivity in an entirely different light. For Alcoff the objective is the real in the sense of having material consequences in the world. But it is not objective in the modernist sense of true and irrefutable. On Alcoff's view there are many ontologies out there in the world. They have consequences; they model reality for us. But none gives us a true one-to-one correspondence to reality.

Visible Identities (2006) develops these themes in more detail. The "visible" in the title refers to the visible marks of identity on the body: race and gender operate through the visibility of bodies. Thus identity is not just

> what is given to an individual or group, but it is also a way of inhabiting, interpreting and working through, both collectively and individually, an objective social location and group history. (2006:42)

In *Real Knowing* (1996) Alcoff turned to Gadamer to articulate her position, and Gadamer also provides the basis for her argument here. Gadamer's perspective, she asserts, rules out an absolute relativism on identity. No horizon of human being on this earth will be totally incommensurable because all humans share a material life. But there is relativism in the valuation of social practice (2006:100). In a bold move, Alcoff applies her understanding of the relationship between objective and relative to the dangerous territory of sexed identity and the body. Her thesis is that there is an objective basis of sexed identity: women and men have a different relationship to the possibility of biological reproduction (172). Relativism enters in the valuation of this relationship.

Although Alcoff defines her approach to identity in terms of the "realism" of Moya and Mohanty, there are significant differences in her account that provide a more viable theory. All of these theorists want to avoid relativism. But while Moya and Mohanty turn to what they see to be the objectivism of Marx, Alcoff turns to Gadamer. Gadamer's perspective avoids relativism, but without retreating to even a circumscribed notion of objective reality. If we define identity as a horizon of meaning from which we know the world, we can posit a social location that is objective without being absolute. In the terminology I am employing here, identities disclose a world for us. This disclosure will differ significantly between different identities. These identities are discursively constituted; I cannot arbitrarily choose the identity I inhabit. But as Alcoff argues so persuasively, they are also real. The material effects of different identities structure the hierarchy of social relations.

I stated at the outset that understanding the subject is the most difficult aspect of an ontology of the social. The foregoing discussion has demonstrated that difficulty. The challenge is to integrate the materiality of bodies that are sexed and raced into the discussion of the subject without losing sight of the power of discursive regimes. My argument here has been that subjects are best understood on the model of Pickering's mangle. Subjects are constituted through the intra-action of discourse, genetically coded bodies, social norms, technology, science, and many other factors. No single factor is causal; all are constitutive. And, as the postpositivist realists argue, the identities that subjects inhabit are real; they have material consequences. But I have argued that these identities are not real in the sense of objectively right or true. Reality is disclosed through our concepts and, most importantly, through my understanding of which subject position I inhabit. The reality this subject position discloses is my reality; other subject positions disclose a different reality. What avoids relativism in this formulation is not that I can declare that one subject position provides a truer picture of reality, but that I can compare the material consequences of the different disclosures. Some subject positions entail privilege, others deny subjects a viable life. These are real differences that can and should be the basis of social critique. As Butler's work so graphically demonstrates, imagining a world in which we have a more inclusive notion of personhood is both a fundamental challenge to social organization and a necessary goal of social change.

An Ontology of the Social

I began this study with a problem: how to bring the material back into the theoretical equation without losing the insights of the linguistic turn that characterized the last decades of the twentieth century. I have focused on theorists who offer a perspective that moves the discussion beyond complaints about the lack of attention to the material in contemporary thought. Bruno Latour, Andrew Pickering, Ludwig Wittgenstein, Michel Foucault, Nancy Tuana, Karen Barad, and the others I have discussed here have articulated positions that understand the relationship between language and the world in exciting new ways. The "settlements" they provide will form the basis for intellectual thought in the twenty-first century.

It should be evident from the foregoing that the strength of the approach lies in its analysis of the natural sciences. Descriptions such as Pickering's mangle and Barad's agentic realism give us a clear picture of how scientists interface with the world through language, technology, politics, and a host of other factors. In retrospect, the clarity of this aspect of the settlement should come as no surprise: those who initially explored these issues were philosophers of science and were primarily interested in the science/world relationship. Another strength of the approach is the work of feminist theorists. Nancy Tuana's new metaphysics,

Karen Barad's intra-actionism, and the work of feminist theorists of the body as well as those who have reopened the question of biology in feminism have revolutionized feminists' understanding of knowledge and the world. Building on the insights of linguistic constructionism, these theorists have not only brought the material back in, they have brought in a whole range of other factors. The work of these theorists demonstrates how the mangle works for bodies in the social world. What we learn from these analyses is that a complex of factors—technological, scientific, material, biological, political, economic, linguistic—intra-act in the constitution of social phenomena. Thus understanding these phenomena—for women and every other member of the social world—requires an understanding of the complexity of these issues and how they participate in the construction of social reality. We must explore the mangle that constitutes the entirety of the social world.

Perhaps the major theme pervading all these discussions is the rejection of dichotomies. If there is one area of agreement among all these thinkers, it is that the root problem of modernity is the dichotomies that define it. The dichotomy between language and the world led to representationalism and the untenable options that it presents. The move to ontology and away from epistemology that characterizes the work of these thinkers definitively rejects representationalism and displaces the dichotomy that informs it. Another key dichotomy that these theorists have challenged is that of nature/culture. The feminist theorists are particularly strong here. Tuana's analysis of Katrina; Barad's examination of the sonogram; the work of Wilson, Kirby, Gatens, and many others displace the nature/culture dichotomy by revealing how the natural and cultural intra-act in ways that make it impossible to clearly distinguish them as separate spheres. These analyses have changed the theoretical landscape of feminism and critical theory more broadly. Since feminists "discovered" gender, the lens of feminist analysis has been fixed exclusively on culture. There has been an almost unchallenged assumption that "woman" is wholly a cultural construct. The theorists I have discussed here have challenged that assumption and in so doing transformed feminist theory.

There is, however, a significant lacuna in these analyses. The feminist theorists of the "new settlement" have challenged the nature/culture distinction by showing how the natural world, either of bodies or the more-than-human world, intra-acts with the cultural. So Tuana gives us an analysis of how global warming, a natural phenomenon caused by political/cultural/economic actions, contributes to the severity of a hurricane that has human and more-than-human effects. And Barad explains how a technological/scientific practice intra-acts with the politics of abortion. But insightful as these analyses are, they are also limited. They describe the intra-action of the human and more-than-human worlds. The ontology that emerges from these analyses is very persuasive. But it raises a question that few of these theorists address: what can we say about the ontology of the strictly social, those things that are defined solely by social practices?

A famous story about the philosopher John Searle speaks to this question. Searle stands in front of his audience waving a dollar bill, asking his listeners to contemplate the meaning of this object. His point, of course, is that the bill's meaning, and hence its existence, is purely social. Unless we constituted the meaning of this object as money, having a particular value and specific social uses, it would cease to have any meaning at all: it would cease to *be*. Searle has had much to say about phenomena such as money in his work. His analysis of speech-acts that create meaning through the use of words in a particular social setting is well known. To say "I do" in the context of a marriage ceremony constitutes the institution of marriage. The words of the man and woman (although, significantly, this is changing) linked to the institutional status of the individual performing the ceremony constitute the marriage. Without these elements, all strictly social, the marriage would not exist.

The social world is constituted in part by phenomena of the same class as marriage. Economic, political, familial, religious, and other institutions are constituted by the concepts through which we understand them. Congress is what it is because we possess a whole set of political concepts and practices that constitute it as a political institution. Without those concepts it could not and would not exist. The theorists who articulate the new settlement have little to say about this class of phenomena. Yet if we succeed in displacing the nature/culture dichotomy, we need to bring these phenomena into our discussions as well. Specifically, we need to consider the ontology of these phenomena. To be consistent, we cannot deny these phenomena ontological status. To do so would be to reify the nature/culture divide we are trying to displace.

The foregoing discussion of identity is an important step in the direction of bringing ontology into the strictly social realm. Butler and Alcoff offer insightful analyses of how the "I" acquires ontological status and the way in which the discursive practices in a society turn bodies into subjects. But there is more to the social sphere than subjects. Subjects exist in social, political, economic, and other institutions. Those institutions, furthermore, are also constitutive of subjects' identities. My identity within the political institutions of my society is partly constituted by how that institution defines citizenship, who is included and who is excluded. This is true of other institutions as well.

It should perhaps not be surprising that the original author of the concept of a new settlement, Bruno Latour, should have taken on the question of the ontology of the social. In *Reassembling the Social* (2005) Latour plunges into the realm of the social, attempting to apply his complex theory of assemblages and collectives here as well. Specifically, he attempts to show why the social cannot be constructed as a kind of material or domain and to dispute the project of providing a social exploration of some state of affairs (2005:1). In an explicit acknowledgment of the limits of his settlement, Latour asserts that he has done much work on the assemblages of nature and that now it is necessary to scrutinize what is assembled under "society." To tackle this problem, Latour begins by asserting that there is nothing specific to the social—there is no "social domain." What Latour attempts to do is to develop what he calls a "sociology of associations," which will enable him to deploy the many controversies about associations without restricting the social to a specific domain (9–16). Following the basic parameters of ANT that he embraced earlier in his career, Latour argues that social scientists should attempt to explain stability in society, not seek it (35).

One of the strengths of Latour's book is his further discussion of an issue that has occupied him in his previous work: construction. Isn't it odd, he notes, that when discussing things like skyscrapers and automobiles we are interested in *how well* they are constructed. Yet when we talk about the construction of facts in social and natural science, we mean that they are not *true* (2005:89–90). His point is clear: the dichotomy between the real and the constructed is, like all dichotomies, a false one. This has important implications for the concept of a social ontology. It entails that, far from being afraid of construction, we should embrace it.

What we learn from Latour's book is, in the end, that the social world, like the natural, is composed of "assemblages." The question of the social emerges when the ties in which we are entangled begin to unravel. What we call the social is the association through many nonsocial entities (2005:247). In a theoretical sense, this is not too different from what emerges in Tuana's analysis of Katrina. But unlike Tuana's analysis, Latour remains entirely in the realm of theory. We don't have a sense of what all these collectives, associations, and assemblages would look like in the real social world. We need much more than Latour's fancy theoretical footwork to bring us closer to a social ontology.

An obvious place to start in the effort to articulate a social ontology is cultural studies—a rich, diverse, and wide-ranging approach that embodies many of the aspects of the new settlements. Cultural studies theorists' interest in culture embraces both the discursive and the material—and, indeed, the interaction between them. Feminist cultural studies, in particular, has been immensely insightful in explicating women's status in contemporary society. Studies such as those of Donna Haraway and Susan Bordo reveal how culture crafts women's bodies, thus erasing the distinction between nature and culture in the constitution of "woman." In short, cultural studies has enhanced our understanding of the social in myriad ways.

There are significant affinities between cultural studies and the new settlements I am examining here. As one commentator on cultural studies remarked, cultural studies is "interdisciplinary, transdisciplinary, and sometimes counterdisciplinary" (Nelson et al. 1992:4). Much the same could be said of the new settlements. Another commonality is the concern with power. Cultural studies theorists are centrally concerned with the interaction between cultural practices and relations of power. The proponents of the new settlements are interested in the intra-action that constitutes knowledge and power in all aspects of human life. In the foregoing analysis, I have relied on the work of feminist cultural studies theorists. In the following examination of Marx, I rely on the work of one of the founding fathers of cultural studies, Stuart Hall. The social ontology I develop is heavily indebted to Marx; much of cultural studies is similarly located.

Despite these affinities, however, I will not define the following in terms of a cultural studies perspective. The reason for this is very simple: I want to explore the social in terms of the discourse developed in the new settlements. The theorists of the new settlements offer a distinctive and productive approach to questions of knowledge and the world. My goal in the following is to apply that discourse to the question of the ontology of the social. My hope is that this analysis will produce a new way of looking at the social that answers questions not addressed in other accounts.

If we want to explore the ontology of the social sphere, the figure that comes immediately to mind is Marx. Marx was insistent on the ontological/material basis of the social world. Marx is commonly interpreted as arguing that the objective reality of the material/economic conditions of society directly cause all other social phenomena. Determination "in the last instance" by the economy is one of the pillars of Marxist theory. The problem here, of course, is that Marx gives us an ontology, but it appears to be a modernist ontology of a fixed, given reality. This is not the "new ontology" of the theorists discussed here, an ontology that is multiple and shifting. It would seem, then, that Marx can be of little help in defining the ontology of the social world we are seeking.

But perhaps we should not dismiss Marx so quickly. Reading Marx across the literature I have been examining here suggests interesting possibilities. Like those seeking a new settlement, Marx discusses the interface of the material and the ideological/linguistic. The accepted interpretation of Marx's understanding of this interface is strict determinism: the material/economic wholly determines the ideological/linguistic. But this is not the only possible interpretation of Marx's work.[9] In an innovative and controversial reading of Marx, Louis Althusser (1969) develops an understanding of the relationship between the material and the ideological/linguistic that has significant parallels to the new settlements. And, most importantly for my purposes, Althusser addresses the institutions that constitute the social world and their ontological status.

The relevance of Althusser's work to that of the contemporary theorists I am discussing lies in the fact that Althusser, like these theorists, is attempting to move away from the strictures of modernity, and in his case, the modernist interpretation of Marx.

What Althusser is trying to do in his commentaries on Marx is to carve out a unique space for Marxist theory. What that space is *not* is easier to specify than what it *is*. He makes it clear that it cannot conform to the empiricism or crude economism of the dominant Marxist interpretations. But there is another element in Althusser's theory that is less obvious yet that structures his approach in important ways. It is crucially important for Althusser to account for the constitutive role of language/ideology in social relations. Like many of his contemporaries, Althusser is deeply concerned with language. But unlike most linguistic constructionists, he is also a Marxist and is thus not willing to entirely relinquish the material in favor of the discursive. The result is that Althusser develops an approach to the material that is unique among his contemporaries, both Marxist and non-Marxist.

It is this idiosyncratic quality that provides the connection between Althusser's theory and contemporary discussions. Reading Althusser across theorists such as Latour and Pickering yields productive results. Althusser is attempting to accomplish two objectives that are particularly relevant to the contemporary effort to find what Latour calls a "new settlement" to the problems posed by modernity. First, Althusser wants to define Marxism as opposed to empiricism, idealism, or materialism. His contention is that Marxism constitutes a "new continent of thought" that represents a repudiation of all aspects of the epistemology of modernity.

Second, Althusser wants to bring language and its constitutive powers into Marxist theory. Like many twentieth-century thinkers, Althusser wants to analyze the role of discourse in the constitution of society. But precisely because he is a Marxist, Althusser never loses sight of the material in his theory. The result is an integration of language and materiality, not a preference for one over the other. These two objectives are closely connected. The crude economism that Althusser is rejecting defined language as merely one element of the superstructure that, like all the other elements, is wholly determined by the economic base. In order to give language more prominence, Althusser had to complicate the base/superstructure relationship in Marxist theory. This complication became the principal focus of his theoretical effort.

At the center of Althusser's interpretation of Marx is his contention that Marx, far from standing Hegel on his head, entirely rejected Hegelian epistemology. Marx's dialectic, Althusser asserts, has a different structure from that of Hegel (1969:93). Marx's conception of the "whole," furthermore, departs from the Hegelian totality in significant ways. For Marx the whole "is constituted by a certain type of complexity, the unity of a *structured whole* containing what can be called levels or instances which are distinct and 'relatively autonomous'" (Althusser and Balibar 1970:97). Although Althusser concludes this description by arguing that the whole is "fixed in the last instance by the economy," it is clear that something very different is going on here. It is also clear that Althusser is attempting to make a clean break with both idealism and materialism as they were conceived in modernist thought.

Althusser's task is to define the "whole," the "totality" that Marx describes in a way that not only sets it apart from Hegel but also posits a relationship between base and superstructure that is not one of strict singular causality. He effects this primarily through his concept of "overdetermination." This term was originally used by Freud to describe the representation of dream thoughts in images privileged by their condensation of a number of thoughts in a single image. Althusser employs the term to describe his complex understanding of the relationship among the elements that constitute social relations. Rejecting on one hand the single causation of the economic and on the other hand the simplistic notion of contradiction and its role in society, Althusser's concept of overdetermination paints a more complicated picture:

> The "contradiction" is inseparable from the total structure of the social body in which it is found, inseparable from its formal *conditions* of existence and even from the instances it governs; it is radically *affected by them*, determining, but also determined in one and the same moment, and determined by the various *levels* and *instances* of the social formation it animates; it might be called *overdetermined in its principle*. (1969:101)

All societies, Althusser claims, are constituted by an infinity of concrete determinations—political laws, religion, custom, habit. None of these determinations is essential; together they do not constitute an "original organic totality" that is the truth of these concrete determinations (102). Overdetermination, Althusser thus concludes, profoundly transforms Hegel's dialectic (104).

It is tempting to describe Althusser's concept of overdetermination as simply an effort to depict society as a system of multiple causation. But much more is going on in this concept. Althusser is compelled to retain Marx's concept of the determination by the economy in the last instance while at the same time rejecting the singular causation of the economic base. His solution to this problem is that Marx asserts the determination in the last instance by the economy but also the relative autonomy of the superstructures and their "specific effectivity." As he puts it so eloquently in *For Marx:* "From the first moment to the last, the lonely hour of the 'last instance' never comes" (1969:113).[10]

Althusser follows this significant statement with the assertion that *"the theory of the specific effectivity of the superstructure and other 'circumstances' largely remains to be elaborated"* (1969:113). Clearly, Althusser sees it as his task to accomplish this elaboration. The overdetermination of any contradiction of an element of a society means, first, that a revolution in the structure does not necessarily modify the existing superstructure and, second, that the new society produced by the revolution may ensure the survival of older elements of the superstructure (115). It should come as no surprise that Althusser uses Lenin's work to develop his position on overdetermination. Lenin was forced to do some fancy theoretical footwork to explain the Russian Revolution in Marxist terms. Without a more complex understanding of the base/superstructure relationship, the Russian Revolution makes little sense. But, Althusser asserts, the lesson of overdetermination emerging from the Russian Revolution is not simply that this event is an exception. Rather, Althusser wants to argue that *all* situations are exceptional; the apparently simple contradiction is always overdetermined (104–6). In general, Althusser concludes, there is no simple transposition of expression between the various instances of the social structure. Rather, the forms vary according to the degree of autonomy of one instance with respect to another (Althusser and Balibar 1970:305–307).

> The absence of the cause in the structure's "metonymic causality" on its effects is not the fault of the exteriority of the structure with respect to economic phenomena; on the contrary, it is the form of the interiority of the structure, as a structure, in its effects. (1970:188)

It is easy to criticize Althusser's concept of overdetermination as unnecessarily complex. But this complexity also offers significant advantages. The most important is a way to talk about the social and social relations from a Marxist perspective that avoids the singular causality of previous interpretations. Society, on Althusser's account, is not simply a product of economic forces. It is an intricate relationship among contradictory and diverse forces that cannot be simply determined by the economy or any other single factor. Another advantage lies in Althusser's concept of "relative autonomy." Social forces are not all the same. They cannot be subsumed under one general theory. Rather, the different social forces, including, most notably, language, must be carefully analyzed *in their autonomy.* This opens up a range of analysis that was closed to previous Marxist theories. In sum, then, Althusser's concept of overdetermination is exceedingly complex because it is an attempt to describe a complex, diverse range of relationships. Like the new settlements, Althusser's theory represents an attempt to explore the complicated relationship among a varied array of factors—the mangle. The advantage of Althusser's theory is that it brings the mangle into the world of social institutions.

There are two other elements of Althusser's interpretation of Marxist theory that are relevant to my concerns here: theoretical production and subjectivity. Althusser's description of theoretical production is at the heart of his understanding of Marx and is central to his reinterpretation. It takes on a pivotal element of Marxism, the relationship between the real and the theoretical, and offers a bold new understanding of that relationship. It is perhaps the most innovative and exciting aspect of Althusser's theory.

Althusser begins his discussion of theoretical production under the rubric of a discussion of "practice." The concept of practice is, of course, one of the focal points of Marxist theory; the unity of theory and practice is one of the basic tenets of Marxist thought. But the "practice" in Althusser's theory constitutes a significant departure from the commonly understood Marxist definition. "Practice," Althusser asserts, is the "*transformation* of a determinate given raw material into a determinate *product,* a transformation effected by a determinate human labor, using determinate means (of 'production')" (1969:166). Althusser defines the determinate moment in this process as the labor of transformation itself. "Social practice," Althusser goes on, is a "complex unity" that contains a large number of particular practices; theoretical practice is only one of them. This definition covers a lot of theoretical ground. "Social practice" is the complex unity out of which the concept of overdetermination arose. It is the heart of Althusser's understanding of Marx's theory, but it is an understanding closer to contemporary social theory than traditional Marxism. It is a concept that allows us to examine the elements of the social structure autonomously, not as solely determined by the economic base.

What, then, is theoretical practice? Theory, Althusser states, is a specific practice that acts on its own object and ends in its own product: knowledge. The raw material of theoretical practice is concepts; the means of production is method (1969:173). Althusser then launches into the heart of this theory, the "Generalities." The process of theoretical practice involves, first, Generalities I, the raw material of science's theoretical practice. Althusser makes it clear from the outset that this raw material is not an objective given. The product of the transformation of Generality I is Generality III, knowledge. Generality II, then, is the theory of the science at any given moment, the method (183–84). "Theoretical practice," Althusser concludes, "produces *Generalities III* by the work of *Generality II* on *Generality I*" (185).

Althusser's clarification of this theory adds, if anything, even more complexities. He insists that there is never an identity of essence between Generality I and Generality III, but always a real transformation. And, most significantly, the movement from Generality I to Generality III is a movement from the abstract to the concrete. It only involves theoretical practice; it takes place entirely in knowledge. Althusser insists that Marx himself defined the correct scientific method as a movement from the abstract to the concrete (1969:185). The "concrete-in-thought" should never be confused with "concrete-reality" (186).

In *Reading Capital*, Althusser and Balibar reflect on this theory in a broader sense. They insist that we must completely reorganize our idea of knowledge, conceiving it strictly as a production. Once more appealing to Marx, they insist that Marx defends the distinction between the real-object (real-concrete), which survives in its independence outside the head, and the object of knowledge, a product of thought that produces it in itself as a thought-concrete. For Marx, they insist, the production process of the object of knowledge takes place completely in knowledge and is carried out according to a different order (1970:41).

For Althusser, what Marx is accomplishing is the opening up of a "new space" in the understanding of knowledge. Western philosophy's "problem of knowledge," he declares, is a "closed circle" (1970:53). For Marx, however, "thought is the historically constituted system of an *apparatus of thought*, founded on and articulated to natural social reality. It is defined by a system of real conditions which make it . . . a determinate *mode of* production of knowledge" (1970:41). In *Lenin and Philosophy* he puts it this way: "Every abstract concept therefore provides knowledge of a reality whose existence it reveals: an 'abstract concept' then means a formula which is apparently abstract but really terribly concrete, because of the object it designates" (2001:49). As an example, Althusser points to the capitalist mode of production. It is invisible to the senses, an abstract concept, yet it is also undeniably concrete and "real" to everyone in a capitalist society. This example gets at the heart of Althusser's theory. Althusser is opposing an empiricism that relies on an objectively given reality. But in doing so, he is not abandoning the real. On the contrary, his whole point is to get at the real-concrete in social relations. His claim is that the theory of Generalities does precisely this.

It is possible that Althusser's theory was meant to be deliberately provocative. He wanted to challenge established Marxist theory by taking on one of its sacred cows: the relationship between theory and practice. Its significance, however, is undeniable. It is, at the very least, an innovative interpretation of Marx. To claim that Marx should be interpreted as providing a theory that moves from the abstract to the concrete is a bold move, forcing us to rethink some of the foundations of Marxist theory. But as Althusser's example of the capitalist mode of production illustrates, it is also a compelling interpretation. Althusser's theory, like that of the new settlements, integrates the discursive and the material in a new way. There are significant affinities between Althusser's theory and that of Latour. Latour wants to challenge our understanding of the constructed and the real; Althusser destabilizes our conception of the abstract and the concrete. Like Latour, Althusser's theory denies the objective reality of the material without denying its reality. It acknowledges the role of the discursive without taking the linguistic turn of many of his contemporaries. Finally, it integrates the role of disciplinary concepts in the production of knowledge. The result is a theory that, in effect, displaces the real/abstract dichotomy.

This same complex understanding of the relationship between language and reality informs the second relevant aspect of Althusser's theory: the subject and its relationship to ideology. Discussions of the subject were everywhere in the work of Althusser's contemporaries. Althusser refers to the work of Foucault and Lacan frequently. His work is deeply influenced by the linguistic approach to the subject that dominates these theories. The discursive constitution of the subject that informs the theories of Lacan and the postmoderns comes out in his theory of "interpellation." Like these theorists, Althusser argues that subjects are constituted by discursive forces; they have no essential identity. But again, Althusser's theory has a distinctive cast. For Althusser, one cannot discuss the subject without the concept of ideology: "All ideology hails or interpellates concrete individuals as concrete subjects" by the functioning of the category of the subject (2001:117). Ideology recruits subjects among individuals (118).

Althusser's theory of ideology is an extension of his argument about Marx's understanding of the complexity and interrelationship of social forces. Althusser distinguishes between two kinds of state apparatuses: repressive state apparatuses (RSA) such as law, courts, and prisons, and ideological state apparatuses (ISA) such as religion, education, family, culture, and communication (2001:96). This distinction in itself is a departure from classical Marxism that subsumes all these institutions under a general concept. But for my purposes it is another aspect of Althusser's discussion that is significant: his claim that ideology has a material existence and that its practice is material (112).[11]

Althusser begins his discussion with what seems to be the standard Marxist interpretation of ideology: ideology represents the imaginary relationship of individuals to their real conditions (2001:109). But then he goes on to link this concept to his understanding of practice. The idea of a human subject exists in the subject's actions, and actions are inserted into practices. Thus the existence of a subject's ideas is material in the sense that

> his ideas are his material actions inserted into material practices governed by material rituals which are themselves defined by the material/ideological apparatus from which derive the ideas of that subject. (114)

Just in case we didn't get the point, Althusser then goes on to assert that ideology exists in "material ideological apparatuses, prescribing material practices governed by material ritual, which practices exist in the material actions of a subject acting in all consciousness according to his belief" (115). What we are left with, then, is the intimate interconnection of ideology, materiality, and subjects: "The category of the subject is only constitutive of all ideology insofar as all ideology has the function (which defines it) of 'constituting' concrete individuals as subjects," and ideology is nothing but its functioning in the material forms of existence of that functioning (116).

Althusser has a specific reason for his iconoclastic interpretation of Marxism: to displace the modernist interpretation and assert a version of Marxism that, quite literally, transforms Western conceptions of knowledge. I would also like to offer an iconoclastic interpretation of Marx. But my purpose is different from that of Althusser. I want to reinterpret Marxist theory in order to develop a social ontology that is compatible with the new settlements I have been examining. To that end I will rely on Althusser's work, using it as a springboard to examine other aspects of Marx's work that move in the direction of a social ontology rooted in this new approach.

One of the themes of the new settlements is the intra-action between the human and the nonhuman world. The modernist interpretation of Marx suggests that his position is the antithesis of this position, that he sees the natural and the social as radically distinct. But as several contemporary theorists have suggested, another interpretation is more supportable. Timothy Luke, for example, argues that if we read Marx through Latour, what we discover is that Marx is concerned with the "multiple links, intersecting influences, and continuous negotiations" between the human and the nonhuman (1999:39). Marx's work, Luke argues, challenges the dichotomy of nature/culture, seeing them not as separate but as one active organic/inorganic product (44). The key passage supporting this interpretation is in Marx's "Economic and Philosophical Manuscripts":

> The universality of man manifests itself in practice in that universality which makes the whole of nature his *inorganic body*, (1) as a direct means of life and (2)

as the matter, the object and the tool of his life activity. Nature is man's *inorganic body*, that is to say nature in so far as it is not the human body. Man *lives* from nature, i.e. nature is his *body*, and he must maintain a continuing dialogue with it if he is not to die. To say that man's physical and mental life is linked to nature simply means that nature is linked to itself, for man is a part of nature. (1992:328)

The theme that Marx pursues here is strikingly similar to that of Latour and the other theorists of the new settlements: the interconnection and inseparability of man and nature. It is by interacting with nature, Marx asserts, that man, as a social creature, makes it his own:

The *human* essence of nature exists only for *social* man; for only here does nature exist for him as a *bond* with other *men*, as his existence for others and their existence for him, as the vital element of human reality. Only here does it exist as the *basis* of his own *human* existence. Only here does his *natural* existence become his *human* existence and nature becomes man for him. *Society* is therefore the perfected unity in essence of man with nature, the true resurrection of nature, the realized naturalism of man and the realized humanism of nature. (1992:349–50)

And, finally:

Nature as nature, i.e. in so far as it is sensuously distinct from the secret sense hidden within it, nature separated, and distinct from these abstractions is *nothing*, a *nothing proving itself to be nothing*, it is *devoid of sense*, or only has the sense of an exteriority to be superseded. (399)

In his discussion of the work of major theorists such as Marx and Weber, David Harvey argues that each of these theorists tends to focus on what he calls the different "moments" in the cognitive map of the social process. Marx is commonly interpreted as focusing on the material moment as, he argues, Foucault is identified with the linguistic. But, Harvey asserts, in both of these cases the assessment is incorrect (1996:78–95). As the above passages from Marx attest, he is better understood as moving freely between the material and the discursive and, indeed, focusing on their interaction and inseparability. Like Latour and Pickering, he is asserting that social man makes nature agentic in a particular way through the man/nature connection.

The essence of this man/nature connection is the activity that Marx defines as the center of human life: labor. Man, Marx claims, must maintain a continuing dialogue with nature if he is not to die. Labor plays a dual role in this dialogue. It creates a bond between man and nature because of the necessity of human labor. But it also creates a bond between man and man. As Marx puts it, "the human essence of nature exists only for *social* man" (1992:349). Society, he asserts, perfects and makes possible the "resurrection" of nature; man is naturalized, and nature is humanized.

In *Dialectics of Nature* Engels elaborates on these themes. Although much of the book is concerned with dialectics and the natural sciences, Engels, like Marx, is also concerned with the man-nature-labor connection. Labor, Engels asserts, is the prime condition for all human existence; labor created man himself (1964:172). The development of labor, furthermore, brought members of a society closer together by increasing mutual support and joint activity. He even traces the origin of language to the necessity of communication in the activity of labor. In the end, Engels concludes, we do not rule over nature, but, with flesh, blood, and brain, belong to nature; we exist in the midst of it (175–83).

But this is just the beginning of the story. In a capitalist society the result of social labor is a new and unique phenomenon: the commodity. If Latour were telling this story, he would call the commodity a hybrid: a man-nature-labor intersection that is both unique to capitalist society and the element that structures our lives in such a society. Pickering would call it a mangle—the intra-action of social, political, economic, and technological forces into a singular entity. Marx's language is different from that of Latour or Pickering, but the message is very similar. He begins his analysis of commodities in *Capital* by asserting that the commodity appears at first sight as a "very trivial thing," easily understood. Analysis shows, however, that it is a very queer thing, "abounding in metaphysical subtleties and theological niceties" (1967:71). In commodities, man, through his industry, changes the forms of the material of nature in a way that is useful to him. He concludes:

> A commodity is therefore a mysterious thing, simply because in it the social character of men's labor appears to them as an objective character stamped upon the product of that labor: because the relation of the producers to the sum total of their own labor is presented to them as a social relation, existing not between themselves, but between the products of their labor. (72)

He goes on to assert that it is only by being exchanged that the products of labor—commodities—acquire one uniform social status, distinct from the varied forms of existence as objects of utility (73).

The commodity, then, is the pivotal element of a capitalist economy. It links man to nature and man to man, but it also creates a new reality—a second nature—in which man in capitalist society must of necessity exist. Commodities are very much hybrids in Latour's sense, but Marx steers the analysis in a political direction by arguing that they are uniquely destructive hybrids. The commodity is the pivotal element of capitalism, and should capitalism become universal, the destructive effects of the commodity would spread to the entire human race. Marx defines his political project as overcoming these destructive effects.[12]

One of the distinctive aspects of the new settlements is their emphasis on technology and its role in the production of knowledge. Pickering, Latour, Barad, and Tuana all argue that the apparatus is a key factor in the process by which knowledge is constructed. It is significant, therefore, that Marx also emphasizes the importance of technology. But while these theorists were interested primarily in the construction of scientific knowledge, Marx is interested in how technological developments construct the social world. He wants to explore how the development of machines in the Industrial Revolution transformed labor and hence structured the world the laborer inhabited.

Marx begins his discussion of technology and the machine in *Capital* in language that is strikingly similar to that of the new settlements:

> Technology discloses man's mode of dealing with Nature, the process of production by which he questions his life, and thereby also lays bare the mode of formation of his social relations, and of the mental conceptions that flow from them. (1967:372)

The history of the evolution of machines that follows this statement focuses on the movement from manual tools to machines. Machines, Marx argues, acquired an independent form, entirely emancipated from the restraints of human strength (378). But this independence also led to a phenomenon that began to haunt capitalism in Marx's day. Only since the introduction of machinery, Marx asserts, has the worker fought against the instrument of labor itself—the machine as the embodiment of capital, the material basis of the capitalist mode of production (427). Marx seems to be implying that the workers somehow understood the transformation of labor effected by the machine and consequently took out their wrath on those machines.

My purpose in looking at Marx's discussions of man and nature, labor, the commodity, and machines/technology is not to paint him as a precursor of the new settlements. Nor is it to argue for an identity between his position and theirs. Althusser notwithstanding, it is hard not to categorize Marx as a modernist. His dialectical method places him squarely in the dichotomous epistemology of modernity. What I am arguing, however, is that there are elements of Marx's thought that can be used as a foundation to construct what I see to be a lacuna in the new settlements: a social ontology. In other words, I am claiming that Marx gives us a place to start in this project, perhaps more so than any other theorist.

I am not alone in seeing aspects of Marx's thought that move beyond the strictures of modernity. In the introduction to their volume *Postmodern Materialism and the Future of Marxist Theory* (1996), Callari and Ruccio assert that Althusser's interpretation of Marx provides a link between postmodernism and Marxism. They argue that what they call Althusser's "aleatory materialism" can be used to recast Marxism in a nonessentialist and nonteleological mode. They conclude:

> We read Marx (and Marxism) as having a primary, primitive or original reference of a world of beings who are differently and irreducibly constituted in social spaces and through processes, in which economic functions are embedded in diverse discursively and politically constructed social relations. (1996:43)

In a similar vein Laclau and Mouffe (1985) argue that we can define a "post-Marxism" that, although rooted in Marx's thought, also moves beyond it in significant ways. Appealing to Gramsci's concept of hegemony, Laclau and Mouffe argue that we should reject the Marxist conception of socialism that rests on the ontological centrality of the working class. Instead, we should define society as a plurality lacking a single unifying principle. The crucial limitation of a left politics, they assert, is that it attempts to define a priori agents of change and privileged points (1985:178–79). What we need instead is a form of politics that affirms the contingency and ambiguity of every "essence" (193).

In order to sketch the outlines of the social ontology I see emerging from this interpretation of Marx's work, I will turn to an analysis cited by Barad in *Meeting the Universe Halfway*—Leela Fernandez's *Producing Workers* (1997). Barad praises Fernandez's analysis for interweaving the perspectives of poststructuralist and Marxist thought to understand the multiple technologies that produce workers in a capitalist industry. For Barad what makes Fernandez's analysis unique is her argument that it is the material conditions on the shop floor in the jute mill she analyzes that produce relations of class, gender, and other forms of cultural identity in the intra-action of humans and machines (Barad 2007:226–30).

Fernandez's concern in *Producing Workers* is the complexity of the production of cultural identities for the workers. Her goal is to move beyond static distinctions between gender, class, ethnicity, culture, politics, and economy. Her thesis is that the definition of the lines that demarcate each sphere involves continual negotiations of power through institutional, discursive, and everyday practices (1997:6). She concludes that class is a social relationship constituted by three central tiers: structure, consciousness, and political identity. It follows that the "working class" is not a homogeneous entity; it is not purely discursive or economically determined but is a result of the intra-action of all these factors (10).

Contesting the homogeneity of "class" and its economic determination is not unique to Fernandez's work. Laclau and Mouffe, along with many cultural studies theorists, make this point. What is unique is her analysis of what she calls "shop-floor politics"—how workers are positioned on the shop floor and how this positioning is contingent on gender and community. Appealing to Foucault's analysis of the techniques of power, Fernandez argues that the system of factory discipline in the jute factory produces particular analytic and material borders between class, gender, and community (1997:59). On one level what Fernandez is doing is positioning herself between a strict economic determinism on one hand and linguistic determinism on the other. Thus she argues that structure does not represent a set of transcendent, objective determinates but is shaped by modes of representation and meaning that social actors give to their positions and activities (136). What sets Fernandez's account apart, however, is her emphasis on an aspect of social life that is one of the pivotal elements of the new settlements: practice. Practice is neither strictly discursive nor strictly material but represents the intra-action between the two. Like Wittgenstein, Fernandez's interest is in what we *do*. In her case this means analyzing what workers do both on the shop floor and in their homes and the integration of these spheres. It is this integration that creates the reality of the workers' lives. As Fernandez concludes, "The representation of social categories and the relationship among these categories have very real political and material effects" (167).

What emerges from Fernandez's account, then, is a mangle. Machinery, discursive practices, economic and political structures intra-act to produce both the bodies and the identities of the workers. Boundaries are fungible, the discursive/material boundary most of all. Agency is everywhere, even in the machines that structure the workers' existence. What Fernandez has accomplished is not just a questioning of the monolithic category of class but an interweaving of all the complex elements that create social reality—ontology—without denying the agentic force of any of these factors.

Elizabeth Grosz argues for the relevance of Darwin for feminist theory and objects to feminists' too-quick dismissal of his work. Feminists' dismissal of Marx has been less thorough, but, especially for feminists trained in postmodernism, Marxist thought has been regarded with deep suspicion. My argument is that we should get over these suspicions. If we are going to bring the real, the material, and the ontological back into our theories and practices, particularly of the social world, then perhaps we should stop being afraid of Marx, a theorist deeply concerned with these issues. A Marxist perspective can lead us to a more complex and comprehensive understanding of the ontology of the specifically social world.

The Marxist social ontology that I am proposing begins with Marx's understanding of the relationship between man and nature, or, in our terminology, between the human and the nonhuman. Although this discussion is cast in terms of the modernist dichotomy between two opposites, it nevertheless points in the direction of a non-dichotomous understanding. Marx's emphasis on labor breaks down the distinction between the human and the nonhuman, the natural and the social. As he sees it, we intra-act with the natural world through labor: nature is man's inorganic body. Furthermore, this intra-action is necessary to sustain human life. As a result, man is naturalized and nature humanized; there is no longer a separation. This intra-action with nature, finally, affects humans' relations with each other: it is through our intra-action with nature that nature exists as a *bond* with others, as a basis for *human* existence. The natural and the social thus merge in human society.

Marx's remarks thus far apply to all human societies in that labor is a commonality of human life. But Marx's principal interest is in a particular form of human society: capitalism. The character of human labor in a capitalist society is unique to that society, and it creates a unique phenomenon: the commodity. The commodity adds another dimension to the man-nature-labor nexus: it creates reality in a capitalist society. The reality of commodities is the foundation of capitalism; the production and consumption of commodities is what capitalism is all about. What a commodity is, what its value is, who produces, consumes, and owns commodities defines what is real in capitalist society. But for Marx commodities are not solely the product of capitalist ideology. They are, rather, both material and discursive, real and ideological objects that, through their absence or presence, create reality for the inhabitants of that society.

Marx's discussion of technology completes his understanding of the mangle that constitutes capitalism. As Fernandez's analysis so effectively illustrates, technology and the machine construct bodies and identities for capitalist workers. As human bodies interact with other human bodies in the presence of machines, identities are created; gender, race, class, and ethnicity are defined; bodies are disciplined. Again, boundaries are vague. It is impossible to clearly demarcate these boundaries, and this is precisely the point of the analysis. The material/discursive, natural/social interaction of these elements is what structures the economic/political reality we call capitalism.

Again, I am not trying to turn Marx into Latour or Pickering. What I am suggesting is that Marx can be read across these theorists very profitably. What emerges is a picture of this social world that displaces the nature/culture dichotomy. Marx's analysis leads us to an understanding of the social world as a product of the intra-action of the natural and the social. But he also gets us to see that the product of that intra-action is a reality that structures our lives and our consciousness. There are several levels of reality here as well as several levels of discourse/ideology. The point is not to try to separate them into neat categories but to analyze their intra-action. In short, it is mangles all the way down.

Marx is concerned primarily with capitalist society and economic relations within that society. But the social ontology suggested by his work can be applied to all aspects of society and any economic system. Following Marx, we can assert that all societies are made up of individuals whose subjecthood is determined in advance by the discursive practices of that society. All societies have some form of economic relations that determine the material location of these subjects. All societies also possess some form of political arrangement that further determines the location and status of subjects. And so on. The point is that in all societies these social arrangements are complexly determined by an array of factors that interact to give that society its particular structure. It also follows that this array of factors cannot be neatly divided into the discursive and the material. Rather, these factors interweave—mangle—into the reality we define as society. John Searle notwithstanding, nothing is *purely* discursive. His dollar bill is, it is true, discursively constituted, but this discursive constitution has overwhelming material effects. Who has money and how much, what is done with the money and for what purposes, is at the center of capitalist society. Once more, the material and the discursive merge.

The foregoing discussion of social ontology completes my exploration of the new settlements that are emerging in contemporary thought. Bringing the insights of the new settlements into the realm of the social is both necessary and significant. It completes the articulation of the conception of knowledge that I am defining in this book.

I have argued that the new settlements provide a conception of knowledge that constitutes an escape from the impasse created by the opposition of discourse and reality without privileging either side of this dichotomy. I have discussed many aspects of that conception in my analysis, focusing particularly on the feminist contributions. I have argued for the advantages of various elements of the settlement. In the end, however, two aspects of the settlements stand out as the most significant: they give us a way to understand knowledge through the concept of the mangle, and they give us a way to assess knowledge through the concept of disclosure.

Mangles mangle. The significant advantage of the mangle is that it allows us to avoid the choice between discourse and reality that has created the current impasse of knowledge. It allows us to understand knowledge as complex and multifaceted. It gives us a tool to break down the components of knowledge and assess their effects. The mangle, however, does not entail a conception of knowledge that is confused and chaotic. On the contrary, it is a tool to understand each of the elements in their complexity, in their autonomy, as Althusser would say, while at the same time giving us means to examine the array of elements that constitute it.

Pickering's mangle originated in the philosophy of science, and its strengths lie there. Pickering, Latour, and especially Barad brilliantly describe how scientific knowledge is constructed through the intra-action of language, material reality, technology, apparatuses, and other factors. Their approach is beginning to transform science studies as well as feminist studies of the body and the reality of women's lives. The advantages of this perspective have become apparent to a broad range of theorists.

My discussion in this chapter is an attempt to bring the mangle into the realm of the social. The challenges here are formidable: how can we conceive the subject as a material reality without slipping back into the Cartesian essential subject? How can we integrate the insights of linguistic constructionism without embracing the concept of the fictive subject? When faced with social institutions the challenges are also significant. Clearly, our concepts constitute institutions such as the economy, political structures, social structures such as the family, and myriad others. But it is also clear that these institutions have material effects.

The perspective of the mangle can address both of these issues. Subjects can *be* only through social norms, but that being is not wholly encompassed by those norms. Subjects have an ontological reality that intra-acts with societal norms. Social institutions, furthermore, are not merely linguistic constructions; they have material effects on the individuals (subjects) who inhabit them. It is also significant that science and technology are a part of both mangles. As Barad's analysis of the sonogram illustrates, scientific and technological apparatuses can have wide-ranging political consequences. Granting the fetus political rights is significantly enhanced by "seeing" it on the screen of the sonogram. Global warming is another example of the workings of the mangle. The scientific evidence for or against global warming will determine, to a great extent, whether political and economic action is taken to combat it.

Mangles, then, are everywhere. They construct the world we inhabit in all its complexity. But we need to do more than understand the constitution of our world—we need to assess it as well. This is where disclosure comes in. The concept of disclosure as I have articulated it here gives us a yardstick by which to compare different realities. The philosophers of science I described above give us a clear picture of how disclosure operates in the construction of scientific reality. Even though they do not employ the term, Pickering, Latour, and Barad explore how different concepts and different technologies disclose different realities. Those realities can be compared and assessed according to their scientific merit.

The concept of disclosure is, if anything, even more useful in the analysis of social reality. Disclosure in the social realm describes the relationship between the material, the discursive, the technological, and the practices they constitute. Social practices disclose reality for us in particular societies. The social practices of Western democracy disclose a reality structured by liberalism, capitalism, patriarchy, science, technology, and many other factors. Social practices of other societies disclose other realities. Disclosures, furthermore, have material effects. The social practices of capitalist society create a reality structured by class, gender, and race. They create a reality of privilege and deprivation, inequality and discrimination.

Disclosure, then, gives us something to examine. Different disclosures yield different material realities. We can weigh the advantages and disadvantages of these different realities and assess their effects. This, of course, is the essence of social critique. What I am suggesting with the concept of disclosure, however, is that it provides an alternative to the two poles of social critique: objectivism and cultural relativism. Disclosures do not reveal truth, but only one version of truth. But this version of truth is a material version that can be compared to other material versions. The trap of cultural relativism is that it leads us to a place where comparison is precluded. Understanding social reality in terms of disclosure, in contrast, leads us to look at the material effects of different social practices and argue for or against them.

There is a closely related aspect to disclosure that is equally important: responsibility and accountability. At the end of *Meeting the Universe Halfway* Barad states: "We need to meet the universe halfway, to take responsibility for the role that we play in the world's differential becoming" (2007:396). Although she does not discuss it in her work, that universe also includes the social reality we inhabit. This social reality is not an arbitrary construction but rather a result of social practices for which we are responsible. Taking responsibility for these practices means, first, understanding their nature and extent, and, second, assessing the material consequences of those practices. It has, in short, an ethical component.

I think that this is the spirit of what Foucault calls the critical ontology of ourselves. That critical ontology must begin with a comprehensive understanding of how our social practices disclose the reality that defines our social existence. This is where the mangle comes in. Foucault is attempting to accomplish this in his studies of prisons, asylums, hospitals, and the evolution of our concept of self. But taking responsibility for our social practices need not stop there. We can imagine and work for other ontologies, other disclosures. Foucault talks about the possibility of going beyond the limits imposed on us, imagining other ways of being that transcend disciplinary society. Butler imagines the possibilities of a concept of subjecthood that is more fluid and inclusive. Imagining other disclosures of social reality entails imagining another material reality, a reality in which subjects' lives would be, in Butler's sense, viable. It suggests a new form of social critique that will be appropriate to the construction of knowledge in the twenty-first century.

NOTES

Introduction

1. See, for example, Derrida's commentary on the concept "9/11" in Borradori (2004).

2. Throughout the manuscript I will use *deconstruction* to mean the breaking down of dichotomies, not Derrida's more narrow understanding of the term.

1. The First Settlement

1. In his 1999 book, Hacking effectively satirizes the social constructionist position by arguing that if everything is a social construction, then the concept loses its effectiveness.

2. In the concluding chapter I will discuss and build on another innovative aspect of Rouse's work: disclosure.

3. In this book Latour uses the term "constitution" to describe modernity. "Settlement" replaces this term in *Pandora's Hope* (1999b).

4. In another context Latour refers to this symmetry between humans and non-humans as a "mythical pragmatogony" (1994:799).

5. In one of his more bizarre efforts, Latour curated an art exhibit, "Iconoclash," that brought together religion, science, and contemporary art in an effort to reveal that social construction *increases* the claim to truth (2002).

6. Another bad boy of science, Michael Serres, performs much the same function.

7. Nancy Tuana's analysis of Katrina (2008) is an excellent example of mangle analysis.

8. I examine this interaction in depth in chapter 4.

2. The Second Settlement

1. For a compatible interpretation see Lovibond (1983).

2. Naomi Scheman uses this aspect of Wittgenstein's philosophy to connect his approach to feminist theory. Both Wittgenstein and feminist theorists, she claims, share a respect for the power and seriousness of human practice and human history (2002:3).

3. The Third Settlement

1. I will challenge this thesis later in the chapter.

2. For a compatible interpretation see Han (2002).

3. I discuss this point at greater length with regard to Butler's position in chapter 5.

4. See Dean (1996) and Gabardi (2001).

5. See Alcoff's analysis of Foucault in *Real Knowing* (1996).

6. The broadening of scope is also evident in Foucault's concern with what he calls "governmentality." This concept covers more than government institutions. It describes a set of practices that encompass every aspect of our practices—social, economic, even familial (1991a).

7. I elaborate on this connection in the final chapter. See his *Remarks on Marx* (1991b).

4. The Fourth Settlement

1. See Hekman (1990, 1999).

2. Haraway notes in passing that Latour is not a feminist, but he might be made into one (1991:248).

3. What is at stake in this controversy is revealed in a collection of feminist critiques of epistemology and science in which the authors argue that the only alternative for feminism is to return to a version of modernity (Pinnick et al. 2003).

4. Clough's reliance on pragmatism, although useful in the context of her argument, is not an avenue I wish to pursue. Rorty's pragmatism relies too exclusively on the linguistic; see "The World Well Lost" in *Consequences of Pragmatism* (1982). Davidson is better, but as I will argue in the following discussion, other theorists offer a more substantive basis for the new settlement.

5. In a note, Clough compares her use of Davidson to Barad's use of Bohr's work. She justifies her choice of Davidson's work on the grounds that it is more thorough (2003:113).

6. Richmond Campbell's *Illusions of Paradox* (1998) is a parallel attempt to give feminism an alternative philosophical basis.

7. Chapter 5 of *Meeting the Universe Halfway* (2007) and Barad 1998.

8. Chapter 4 of *Meeting the Universe Halfway* (2007) and Barad 2003.

9. For a similar critique, see Teresa Ebert, *Ludic Feminism and After* (1996).

10. Barad offers a parallel analysis of the production of knowledge and identity in her discussion of Leela Fernandez's *Producing Workers* (1997). Once again her emphasis is on the way multiple technologies produce the identity of, in this case, workers in a

jute mill. Her thesis is that the material conditions on the shop floor produce relations of class and other forms of cultural identity in the intra-action of humans and machines (2007:227). I will discuss this in more detail in chapter 5.

11. Several other theorists have examined this relationship between the political identity of the fetus and the scientific/technological practices to which it is subjected. Monica Casper (1998) analyzes how the development of fetal surgery not only facilitated the understanding of the fetus as an autonomous being but also had the effect of erasing the pregnant woman. In fetal surgery, the mother becomes the passive container of the fetus, who is now active and agentic—the fetal patient. Like Barad, Casper argues that the unborn patient is not a natural phenomenon but a social and cultural achievement. She also argues that this development has political consequences: "The more fetuses are defined as people, the greater the threats to women's reproductive autonomy including abortion rights, decision making in health care settings, and everyday behavior during pregnancy" (1998:215). See also Morgan (2006).

12. For a pragmatist account of the link between objectivity and responsibility, see Lisa Heldke and Stephen Kellert (1995).

13. It is important to distinguish the "new materialism" from "materialist feminism." Although materialist feminism as formulated by Rosemary Hennessy (1993) is sympathetic to postmodernism, it retains a Marxist commitment to the language/reality dichotomy that is antithetical to the new materialism.

14. See her exchange with Butler in Bordo (1998).

15. For a compatible analysis, see Emily Martin's *Flexible Bodies* (1994). In *Philosophy in the Flesh* (1999) George Lakoff and Mark Johnson advance an argument that attacks the mind/body dualism from a different perspective. Lakoff and Johnson assert that the mind is inherently embodied, that abstract concepts are largely metaphysical, and that those metaphors are rooted in the facts of our bodily existence. They take on nothing less than the entire tradition of Western philosophy, suggesting that their insights provide the basis for the redefinition of that tradition. Like the theorists discussed here, they reject representationalism. Their alternative is a theory of truth rooted in the facts of our bodily existence. Although it is doubtful that philosophers will take up Lakoff and Johnson's radical suggestion, they nevertheless represent another indication of the discontent with the dualism of modernist thought that characterizes many contemporary discussions.

5. From Construction to Disclosure

1. For an interesting analysis of the reality of the fetus, see Boltanski (2002).

2. See my analysis of this issue (Hekman 2004:19).

3. Many theorists have argued that Butler abandons linguistic constructionism in *Bodies That Matter*.

4. What is considered "human" and the consequences for those who fall outside this definition is also Butler's concern in *Precarious Life: The Power of Mourning and Violence* (2004b).

5. In a related work Butler even argues that in the later Foucault there is a movement from a discursive notion of the subject to a notion of the self, an entity that carries more agency. This self, she claims, is self-forming but within the practices available to it (2004b:226).

6. I explain this interaction in detail in my *Private Selves/Public Identities* (2004).

7. Many of these scholars are affiliated through the Future of Minority Studies Project. See also Alcoff et al. (2006).

8. See also Wilkerson 2000.

9. In an interesting but rarely cited analysis, Carol Gould (1978) discusses what she calls Marx's social ontology. Like Althusser, Gould posits a more complex relationship between the economic and the ideological than that asserted by the crude economists.

10. Stuart Hall (1996:45) suggests that a better reading of Marx on this point is determination by the economic in the *first* instance.

11. This is a point echoed throughout cultural studies.

12. See Luke (1999:39–42); Gareau (2005:128).

References

Alcoff, Linda. 1996. *Real Knowing: New Versions of the Coherence Theory.* Ithaca, N.Y.: Cornell University Press.

———. 2000. "Who's Afraid of Identity Politics?" In *Reclaiming Identity: Realist Theory and the Predicament of Postmodernism,* ed. Paula Moya et al., 312–44. Berkeley: University of California Press.

———. 2006. *Visible Identities: Race, Gender, and the Self.* New York: Oxford University Press.

Alcoff, Linda, et al., eds. 2006. *Identity Politics Reconsidered.* New York: Palgrave-Macmillan.

Antony, Louise, and Charlotte Witt, eds. 2002. *A Mind of One's Own: Feminist Essays on Reason and Objectivity.* Boulder, Colo.: Westview.

Althusser, Louis. 1969. *For Marx.* Translated by Ben Brewster. London: Verso.

———. 2001. *Lenin and Philosophy and Other Essays.* New York: Monthly Review Press.

Althusser, Louis, and Etienne Balibar. 1970. *Reading Capital.* London: Verso.

Barad, Karen. 1996. "Meeting the Universe Halfway." In *Feminism, Science, and the Philosophy of Science,* ed. Lynn Hankinson Nelson and Jack Nelson, 161–94. Dordrecht: Kluwer.

———. 1998. "Agential Realism: Feminist Interventions in Understanding Scientific Practices." In *The Science Studies Reader,* ed. Mario Biagioli, 1–11. New York: Routledge.

———. 2001. "Scientific Literacy—Agential Literacy=(Learning+Doing) Science Responsibly." In *Feminist Science Studies: A New Generation,* ed. Maralee Mayberry et al., 226–46. New York: Routledge.

———. 2003. "Posthumanist Performativity: Toward an Understanding of How Matter Comes to Matter." *Signs* 28 (3): 801–31.

———. 2007. *Meeting the Universe Halfway: Quantum Physics and the Entanglement of Matter and Meaning.* Durham, N.C.: Duke University Press.

Barnes, Barry 1982. *T. S. Kuhn and Social Science.* New York: Columbia University Press.

———. 2001. "Practice as Collective Action." In *The Practice Turn in Contemporary Theory*, ed. Theodore Schatzki et al., 17–28. New York: Routledge.

Bhaskar, Roy. 1979. *The Possibility of Naturalism*. Atlantic Highlands, N.J.: Humanities Press.

Bloor, David. 1997. *Wittgenstein: Rules and Institutions*. London: Routledge.

Boltanski, Luc. 2002. "The Fetus and the Image War." In *Iconoclash*, ed. Bruno Latour and Peter Weikel, 78–81. Karlsruhe: ZKM/Karlsruhe Publications Program.

Bordo, Susan. 1993. *Unbearable Weight: Feminism, Western Culture, and the Body*. Berkeley: University of California Press.

———. 1998. "Bringing Body to Theory." In *Body and Flesh*, ed. Donn Welton, 84–97. Oxford: Blackwell.

Borradori, Giovanna. 2004. *Philosophy in a Time of Terror: Dialogues with Jurgen Habermas and Jacques Derrida*. Chicago: University of Chicago Press.

Braidotti, Rosi. 2002. *Metamorphoses: Toward a Materialist Theory of Becoming*. Cambridge: Polity Press.

Bray, Elizabeth, and Claire Colebrook. 1998. "The Haunted Flesh: Corporeal Feminism and the Politics of (Dis)embodiment. *Signs* 24 (1): 35–67.

Butler, Judith. 1987. *Subjects of Desire*. New York: Columbia University Press.

———. 1990. *Gender Trouble*. New York: Routledge.

———. 1993. *Bodies That Matter*. New York: Routledge.

———. 1997. *The Psychic Life of Power*. Stanford, Calif.: Stanford University Press.

———. 1999. *Gender Trouble*, 2nd ed. New York: Routledge.

———. 2004a. "Bodies and Power Revisited." In *Feminism and the Final Foucault*, ed. Dianna Taylor and Karen Vintges, eds., 183–94. Urbana: University of Illinois Press.

———. 2004b. *Precarious Life: The Power of Mourning and Violence*. New York: Verso.

———. 2004c. *Undoing Gender*. New York: Routledge.

———. 2005a. *Giving an Account of Oneself*. New York: Fordham University Press.

———. 2005b. "'There Is a Person Here': An Interview with Judith Butler." In *Butler Matters*, ed. Margaret Breen and Warren Blumenfeld, 9–25. Hampshire: Ashgate.

Callari, Antonio, and David Ruccio. 1996. Introduction to *Postmodern Materialism and the Future of Marxist Theory*. Middletown, Conn.: Wesleyan University Press.

Campbell, Richmond. 1998. *Illusions of Paradox: A Feminist Epistemology Naturalized*. Lanham, Md.: Rowman and Littlefield.

Casper, Monica. 1998. *The Making of the Unborn Patient: A Social Anatomy of Fetal Surgery*. New Brunswick, N.J.: Rutgers University Press.

Cavell, Stanley. 1979. *The Claim of Reason*. New York: Oxford University Press.

Clough, Sharyn. 2003. *Beyond Epistemology: A Pragmatist Approach to Feminist Science Studies*. Lanham, Md.: Rowman and Littlefield.

Colebrook, Claire. 2000. "From Radical Representation to Corporeal Becomings: The Feminist Philosophy of Lloyd, Grosz, and Gatens." *Hypatia* 15 (2): 76–93.

———. 2002. *Giles Deleuze*. New York: Routledge.

Connolly, William. 1995. *The Ethos of Pluralization*. Minneapolis: University of Minnesota Press.

———. 2002. *Neuropolitics*. Minneapolis: University of Minnesota Press.

Davidson, Donald. 2001. "Reality without Reference." In *Inquiries into Truth and Interpretation*, 2nd ed., 215–25. Oxford: Clarendon Press.

Dean, Mitchell. 1996. "Foucault, Government, and the Enfolding of Authority." In *Foucault and Political Reason,* ed. Andrew Barry et al., 209–29. Chicago: University of Chicago Press.

Deleuze, Giles. 1987. *Dialogues.* London: Athlone.

———. 1988. *Foucault.* Minneapolis: University of Minnesota Press.

———. 1994. *Difference and Repetition.* Translated by Paul Patton. New York: Columbia University Press.

Deleuze, Giles, and Felix Guattari. 1987. *A Thousand Plateaus: Capitalism and Schizophrenia.* Translated by Brian Massumi. Minneapolis: University of Minnesota Press.

Di Stefano, Christine. 1987. "Postmodernism/Postfeminism? The Case of the Incredible Shrinking Woman." Paper presented at the annual meeting of the American Political Science Association.

Dreyfus, Hubert, and Paul Rabinow. 1982. *Michel Foucault: Beyond Structuralism and Hermeneutics.* Chicago: University of Chicago Press.

Ebert, Teresa. 1996. *Ludic Feminism and After.* Ann Arbor: University of Michigan Press.

Engels, Frederick. 1964. *Dialectics of Nature.* Edited by Clemens Dutt. Moscow: Progress Publishers.

Fausto-Sterling, Anne. 2000. *Sexing the Body: Gender Politics and the Construction of Sexuality.* New York: Basic Books.

———. 2005. "The Bare Bones of Sex: Part 1—Sex and Gender." *Signs* 30 (2): 1491–527.

Fernandez, Leela. 1997. *Producing Workers: The Politics of Gender, Class, and Culture in the Calcutta Jute Mills.* Philadelphia: University of Pennsylvania Press.

Fine, Arthur. 1986. *The Shaky Game: Einstein, Realism, and Quantum Theory.* Chicago: University of Chicago Press.

Foucault, Michel. 1965. *Madness and Civilization: A History of Insanity in the Age of Reason.* New York: Random House.

———. 1970. *The Order of Things.* New York: Random House.

———. 1972a. *The Archaeology of Knowledge.* Translated by A. M. Sheridan Smith. New York: Harper and Row.

———. 1972b. "Discourse on Language." In *The Archaeology of Knowledge,* trans. A. M. Sheridan Smith. New York: Harper and Row.

———. 1973. *The Birth of the Clinic.* New York: Pantheon.

———. 1977. *Language, Countermemory, Practice.* Edited by Donald Bouchard. Ithaca, N.Y.: Cornell University Press.

———. 1979. *Discipline and Punish.* Translated by Alan Sheridan. New York: Random House.

———. 1980a. *The History of Sexuality,* vol. 1. Translated by Robert Hurley. New York: Random House.

———. 1980b. *Power/Knowledge.* New York: Pantheon.

———. 1984. *The Foucault Reader.* Edited by Paul Rabinow. New York: Pantheon.

———. 1985. *The Uses of Pleasure.* New York: Pantheon.

———. 1986. *The Care of the Self.* New York: Pantheon.

———. 1988a. *Politics, Philosophy, Culture: Interviews and Other Writings 1977–1984.* Edited by Lawrence Kritzman. New York: Routledge.

———. 1988b. *Technologies of the Self: A Seminar with Michel Foucault.* Edited by Luther Martin et al. Amherst: University of Massachusetts Press.

———. 1991a. *The Foucault Effect*. Edited by Graham Burchell et al. Chicago: University of Chicago Press.

———. 1991b. *Remarks on Marx*. New York: Semiotexte.

———. 2003. *"Society Must Be Defended."* Edited by Mauro Bertani and Alessandro Fontana. New York: Picador.

Garbardi, Wayne. 2001. *Negotiating Postmodernism*. Minneapolis: University of Minnesota Press.

Gareau, Brian. 2005. "We Have Never Been Human: Agential Nature, ANT, and Marxist Political Ecology." *Capitalism, Nature, Socialism* 16 (4): 127–40.

Garver, Newton. 1990. "Form of Life in Wittgenstein's Later Philosophy." *Dialectica* 44 (1–2): 175–201.

Gatens, Moira. 1996. *Imaginary Bodies: Ethics, Power, and Corporeality*. New York: Routledge.

Gould, Carol. 1978. *Marx's Social Ontology*. Cambridge, Mass.: MIT Press.

Grosz, Elizabeth. 1994. *Volatile Bodies: Toward a Corporeal Feminism*. Bloomington: Indiana University Press.

———. 1995. *Space, Time, and Perversion: Essays on the Politics of Bodies*. New York: Routledge.

———. 2004. *The Nick of Time: Politics, Evolution, and the Untimely*. Durham, N.C.: Duke University Press.

———. 2005. *Time Travels: Feminism, Nature, Power*. Durham, N.C.: Duke University Press.

Hacking, Ian. 1983. *Representing and Intervening*. Cambridge: Cambridge University Press.

———. 1992. "The Self-Vindication of the Laboratory Sciences." In *Science as Practice and Culture*, ed. Andrew Pickering, 29–64. Chicago: University of Chicago Press.

———. 1999. *The Social Construction of What?* Cambridge, Mass.: Harvard University Press.

Hall, Stuart. 1996. *Critical Dialogues in Cultural Studies*. Edited by David Morley and Kuan-Hsing Chen. New York: Routledge.

Han, Beatrice. 1998/2002. *Foucault's Critical Project: Between the Transcendental and the Historical*. Translated by Edward Pile. Stanford, Calif.: Stanford University Press.

Haraway, Donna. 1990. "A Manifesto for Cyborgs: Science, Technology, and Socialist Feminism in the 1980s." In *Feminism/Postmodernism*, ed. Linda Nicholson, 190–233. New York: Routledge.

———. 1991. *Simians, Cyborgs, and Women: The Reinvention of Nature*. New York: Routledge.

———. 1997. *Modest-Witness@Second-Millennium—Female Man-Meets-Onco-Mouse: Feminism and Technoscience*. New York: Routledge.

Harding, Sandra. 2004. "A Socially Relevant Philosophy of Science? Resources from Standpoint Theory's Controversality." *Hypatia* 19 (1): 25–47.

Hardt, Michael. 1993. *Giles Deleuze: An Apprenticeship in Philosophy*. Minneapolis: University of Minnesota Press.

Harvey, David. 1996. *Justice, Nature, and the Geography of Difference*. Oxford: Blackwell.

Hekman, Susan 1990. *Gender and Knowledge*. Boston: Northeastern University Press.

——. 1998. "Material Bodies." In *Body and Flesh*, ed. Donn Welton, 61–70. Oxford: Blackwell.

——. 1999. *The Future of Differences*. Cambridge: Polity Press.

——. 2004. *Private Selves, Public Identities*. University Park: Penn State Press.

Heldke, Lisa, and Stephen Kellert. 1995. "Objectivity as Responsibility." *Metaphilosophy* 26 (4): 360–78.

Hennessy, Rosemary. 1993. *Materialist Feminism and the Politics of Discourse*. New York: Routledge.

Hird, Myra. 2004. *Sex, Gender, and Science*. New York: Palgrave.

Kirby, Vicki. 1997. *Telling Flesh: The Substance of the Corporeal*. New York: Routledge.

Knorr-Certina, Karin. 1992. "The Couch, the Cathedral and the Laboratory." In *Science as Practice and Culture*, ed. Andrew Pickering, 113–38. Chicago: University of Chicago Press.

——. 1999. *Epistemic Cultures: How the Sciences Make Knowledge*. Cambridge, Mass.: Harvard University Press.

Kuhn, Thomas. 1962. *The Structure of Scientific Revolutions*. Chicago: University of Chicago Press.

Kukla, Rebecca. 2006. "Introduction: Maternal Bodies." *Hypatia* 21 (1): vii–ix.

Laclau, Ernesto, and Chantal Mouffe. 1985. *Hegemony and Socialist Strategy*. London: Verso.

Lakoff, George, and Mark Johnson. 1999. *Philosophy in the Flesh: The Embodiment of Mind and Its Challenge to Western Thought*. New York: Basic Books.

Latour, Bruno. 1993. *We Have Never Been Modern*. Translated by Catherine Porter. Cambridge, Mass.: Harvard University Press.

——. 1994. "Pragmatogonies: A Mythical Account of How Humans and Nonhumans Swap Properties." *American Behavioral Scientist* 37 (6): 791–808.

——. 1999a. "On Recalling ANT." In *Actor Network Theory and After*, ed. John Law and John Hassard, 15–25. Oxford: Blackwell.

——. 1999b. *Pandora's Hope: Essays on the Reality of Science Studies*. Cambridge, Mass.: Harvard University Press.

——. 2002. "What Is Iconoclash? Or Is There a World beyond the Image Wars? " In *Iconoclash*, ed. Bruno Latour and Peter Weibel, 14–37. Karlsruhe: ZKM/Karlsruhe Publication Program.

——. 2003. "The Promises of Constructivism." In *Chasing Technoscience: Matrix for Materiality*, ed. Don Ihde and Evan Selinger, 27–46. Bloomington: Indiana University Press.

——. 2004. "Why Has Critique Run Out of Steam? From Matters of Fact to Matters of Concern." *Critical Inquiry* 30 (2): 225–48.

——. 2005. *Reassembling the Social: An Introduction to Actor Network Theory*. Oxford: Oxford University Press.

Latour, Bruno, and Steve Woolgar. 1986. *Laboratory Life*. Princeton, N.J.: Princeton University Press.

Law, John. 1994. *Organizing Modernity*. Oxford: Blackwell.

——. 1999. "After ANT: Complexity, Naming and Topology." In *Actor Network Theory and After*, ed. John Law and John Hassard, 1–14. Oxford: Blackwell.

Longino, Helen. 2002. *The Fate of Knowledge*. Princeton, N.J.: Princeton University Press.

Lovibond, Sabina. 1983. *Realism and Imagination in Ethics.* Minneapolis: Minnesota University Press.

Luke, Timothy. 1999. *Capitalism, Democracy, and Ecology: Departing from Marx.* Urbana: University of Illinois Press.

Lynch, Michael. 1992. "Extending Wittgenstein: The Pivotal Move from Epistemology to Sociology of Science." In *Science as Practice and Culture,* ed. Andrew Pickering, 215–65. Chicago: University of Chicago Press.

Martin, Emily. 1994. *Flexible Bodies: Tracking Immunity in American Culture—from the Days of Polio to the Age of AIDS.* Boston: Beacon Press.

Marx, Karl. 1967. *Capital, Volume 1.* New York: International Publishers.

———. 1992. "Economic and Philosophical Manuscripts." In *Early Writings,* 279–400. London: Penguin.

Massumi, Brian. 1987. Translator's Foreword. In Giles Deleuze and Felix Guattari, *A Thousand Plateaus,* trans. Brian Massumi. Minneapolis: University of Minnesota Press.

McWhorter, Ladelle. 1999. *Bodies and Pleasures: Foucault and the Politics of Sexual Normalization.* Bloomington: Indiana University Press.

Mohanty, Satya. 1997. *Literary Theory and the Claims of History.* Ithaca, N.Y.: Cornell University Press.

———. 2000. "The Epistemic Status of Cultural Identity." In *Reclaiming Identity: Realist Theory and the Predicament of Postmodernism,* ed. Paula Moya and Michael Hames-Garcia, 29–66. Berkeley: University of California Press.

Moi, Toril. 1999. *What Is a Woman? and Other Essays.* Oxford: Oxford University Press.

Mol, Annemarie. 1999. "Ontological Politics: A Word and Some Questions." In *Actor Network Theory and After,* ed. John Law and John Hassard, 74–89. Oxford: Blackwell.

———. 2002. *The Body Multiple: Ontology in Medical Practice.* Durham, N.C.: Duke University Press.

Morgan, Lynn. 2006. "Strange Anatomy: Gertrude Stein and the Avant-Garde Embryo." *Hypatia* 21 (1): 15–34.

Moya, Paula. 2000a. Introduction to *Reclaiming Identity,* ed. Paula Moya and Michael Hames-Garcia, 1–26. Berkeley: University of California Press.

———. 2000b. "Postmodernism, 'Realism,' and the Politics of Identity." In *Reclaiming Identity,* ed. Paula Moya and Michael Hames-Garcia, 67–101. Berkeley: University of California Press.

Moya, Paula, and Michael Hames-Garcia, eds. 2000. *Reclaiming Identity.* Berkeley: University of California Press.

Nelson, Lynn Hankinson, and Alison Wylie. 2004. Introduction. *Hypatia* 19 (1): vii–xiii.

Nelson, Cary, et al. 1992. "Cultural Studies: An Introduction." In *Cultural Studies,* ed. Lawrence Grossberg et al., 1–22. New York: Routledge.

O'Grady, Paul. 2004. "Wittgenstein and Relativism." *International Journal of Philosophical Studies* 12 (3): 315–37.

Orr, Deborah. 2002. "Developing Wittgenstein's Picture of the Soul: Toward a Feminist Spiritual Erotics." In *Feminist Interpretations of Ludwig Wittgenstein,* ed. Naomi Scheman and Peg O'Connor, 322–43. University Park: Penn State Press.

Pickering, Andrew. 1984. *Constructing Quarks.* Chicago: University of Chicago Press.

——. 1995. *The Mangle of Practice: Time, Agency, and Science.* Chicago: University of Chicago Press.

Pinnick, Cassandra, et al., eds. 2003. *Scrutinizing Feminist Epistemology: An Examination of Gender in Science.* New Brunswick, N.J.: Rutgers University Press.

Prado, C. G. 2000. *Starting with Foucault: An Introduction to Genealogy,* 2nd ed. Boulder, Colo.: Westview.

Putnam, Hilary. 1990. *Realism with a Human Face.* Cambridge, Mass.: Harvard University Press.

Read, Rupert. 2002. "Culture, Nature, Ecosystem (or Why Nature Can't Be Naturalized)." In *Feminist Interpretations of Ludwig Wittgenstein,* ed. Naomi Scheman and Peg O'Connor, 408–31. University Park: Penn State Press.

Rorty, Richard. 1979. *Philosophy and the Mirror of Nature.* Princeton, N.J.: Princeton University Press.

——. 1982. *Consequences of Pragmatism.* Minneapolis: University of Minnesota Press.

Rouse, Joseph. 1987. *Knowledge and Power: Toward a Political Philosophy of Science.* Ithaca, N.Y.: Cornell University Press.

——. 1996. *Engaging Science: How to Understand Its Practices Philosophically.* Ithaca, N.Y.: Cornell University Press.

——. 2002. *How Scientific Practices Matter: Reclaiming Philosophical Naturalism.* Chicago: University of Chicago Press.

——. 2004. "Barad's Feminist Naturalism." *Hypatia* 19 (1): 142–61.

Schatzki, Theodore. 1996. *Social Practices: A Wittgensteinian Approach to Human Activity and the Social.* New York: Cambridge University Press.

——. 2001. Introduction to *The Practice Turn in Contemporary Theory,* ed. Theodore Schatzki et al., 1–14. New York: Routledge.

Scheman, Naomi. 2002. Introduction to *Feminist Interpretations of Ludwig Wittgenstein,* ed. Naomi Scheman and Peg O'Connor, 1–21. University Park: Penn State Press.

Searle, John. 1995. *Construction of Social Reality.* New York: Free Press.

Sewell, William. 2001. "Whatever Happened to the 'Social' in Social History?" In *Schools of Thought,* ed. Joan Scott and Debra Keates, 209–26. Princeton, N.J.: Princeton University Press.

Shapin, Steven, and Simon Schaffer. 1985. *Leviathan and the Air Pump: Hobbes, Boyle, and the Experimental Life.* Princeton, N.J.: Princeton University Press.

Stengers, Isabelle. 1997. *Power and Invention: Situating Science.* Minneapolis: University of Minnesota Press.

Tuana, Nancy. 1983. "Re-fusing Nature/Nurture." *Hypatia,* special issue of *Women's Studies International Forum* 6 (6): 45–56.

——. 2001. "Material Locations." In *Engendering Rationalities,* ed. Nancy Tuana and Sandi Morgen, 221–43. Bloomington: Indiana University Press.

——. 2008. "Viscous Porosity: Witnessing Katrina." In *Material Feminisms,* ed. Stacy Alaimo and Susan Hekman, 188–213. Bloomington: Indiana University Press.

Valverde, Mariana. 2004. "Experience and Truth Telling in a Posthumanist World: A Foucaultian Contribution to Feminist Ethical Reflections." In *Feminism and the Final Foucault,* ed. Diana Taylor and Karen Vintges, 67–90. Urbana: University of Illinois Press.

White, Stephen. 2000. *Sustaining Affirmation: The Strengths of Weak Ontology in Political Theory.* Princeton, N.J.: Princeton University Press.

Wilkerson, William. 2000. "Is There Something You Need to Tell Me? Coming Out and the Ambiguity of Experience." In *Reclaiming Identity*, ed. Paula Moya and Michael Hames-Garcia, 251–78. Berkeley: University of California Press.

Wilson, Elizabeth. 1998. *Neural Geographies: Feminism and the Microstructure of Cognition.* New York: Routledge.

———. 1999. "Introduction: Somatic Compliance—Feminism, Biology, and Science." *Australian Feminist Studies* 14 (29): 7–18.

Winch, Peter. 1958. *The Idea of a Social Science and Its Relation to Philosophy.* London: Routledge and Kegan Paul.

———. 1972. *Ethics and Action.* London: Routledge and Kegan Paul.

Wittgenstein, Ludwig. 1958. *Philosophical Investigations.* New York: Macmillan.

———. 1960. *The Blue and Brown Books,* 2nd ed. New York: Harper and Row.

———. 1961. *Tractus Logico-Philosophicus.* Translated by D. F. Pears and B. F. McGuiness. London: Routledge.

———. 1969. *On Certainty.* Edited by G. E. M. Anscombe and G. H. von Wright. New York: Harper and Row.

———. 1970. *Zettel.* Edited by G. E. M. Anscombe and G. H. von Wright. Berkeley: University of California Press.

———. 1974. *Philosophical Grammar.* Edited by Rush Rhees. Berkeley: University of California Press.

———. 1977. *Remarks on Color.* Edited by G. E. M. Anscombe. Berkeley: University of California Press.

———. 1978. *Remarks on the Foundation of Mathematics,* rev. ed. Edited by G. H. von Wright, Rush Rhees, and G. E. M. Anscombe. Cambridge, Mass.: MIT Press.

INDEX

absence, 114; commodity of, 124
actor network theory (ANT), 14–15, 22.
    See also Latour, Bruno
agency, 2, 99, 105, 123, 131n5; and
    hybrids, 19; materiality of, 22–24; and
    reality, 73–74. *See also* Barad, Karen
agential realism, 68, 72–76, 79. *See also*
    Barad, Karen, intra-action
Alcoff, Linda, 28–31, 105–106, 109,
    130n3:5
Althusser, Louis, 64, 111–117, 121–122,
    126, 132n9
analytic philosophy, 6, 28–31
anthropological studies. *See*
    anthropology
anthropology, 4, 44, 98
assemblage, 20, 48–49, 110; and sexed
    bodies, 82
autonomy, 114–115; of the fetus, 78,
    131n11. *See also* Barad, Karen

Barad, Karen, 3, 63, 70; agential realism,
    68, 72–80, 107; discourse, 80, 88–91,
    110, 117, 119, 125–126; intra-action, 31,
    82, 122, 127, 130nn4:7,8; materiality,
    84–85, 90, 93, 105; sonogram technol-
    ogy, 89, 92, 108, 121, 126, 131n11

Barbin, Herculine, 94–95
Barnes, Barry, 11, 13–14
becoming, 49; differential, 76, 79, 127
biological essentialism, 84
biology, 50, 61; in feminist theory, 83–85;
    and society, 44, 80; and women's
    experience, 3
Bloor, David, 11
body: in assemblage, 48, 82; in feminist
    theory, 29, 39, 50, 83–84, 89, 95–96,
    100 (*see also* Butler, Judith); gendered,
    81, 99, 106; inorganic, 118–119, 124 (*see
    also* Marx, Karl); in the mangle, 15,
    107–108, 123–124, 126; materiality of,
    6, 39, 50, 67, 76, 88, 106; ontology of,
    82; in power relations, 53–57 (*see also*
    Foucault, Michel); as practice, 44, 58;
    as subject, 95, 100, 109; of women, 3,
    25–26, 66, 80, 110–111
Bohr, Niels, 73, 130
Bordo, Susan, 6, 80, 110–111
Boyle, Robert, 18, 24
Butler, Judith, 6, 94, 107, 109, 128,
    130n3:3, 131nn14,5:3,4,5; feminist
    critique of, 75–76, 80–81; and ontology
    of the subject, 95–101. *See also*
    Foucault, Michel

Susan Hekman is Professor of Political Science and Director of Graduate Humanities at the University of Texas at Arlington. She is author of *Private Selves, Public Identities* and *The Future of Differences*. She has edited *Feminist Interpretations of Michel Foucault* and (with Stacy Alaimo) *Material Feminisms* (Indiana University Press, 2008).

Printed and bound by CPI Group (UK) Ltd, Croydon, CR0 4YY

13/04/2025

14656551-0004